P9-BBT-803

boy meets girl

JOSHUA HARRIS

Multnomah Books

BOY MEETS GIRL
published by Multnomah Books
© 2000, 2005 by Joshua Harris
International Standard Book Number: 978-1-59052-167-0
Cover photo by David Sacks
Interior design and typeset by Katherine Lloyd, The DESK
Unless otherwise indicated, Scripture references are from:
The Holy Bible, New International Version © 1973, 1984 by International
Bible Society, used by permission of Zondervan Publishing House
Also quoted are:
Holy Bible, New Living Translation (NLT) © 1996. Used by permission
of Tyndale House Publishers, Inc. All rights reserved.
The Message © 1993 by Eugene H. Peterson
Published in the United States by WaterBrook Multnomah, an imprint of
the Crown Publishing Group, a division of Random House Inc., New York.
MULTNOMAH and its mountain colophon are registered trademarks
of Random House Inc.

Printed in the United States of America

ALL RIGHTS RESERVED
No part of this publication may be reproduced, stored in a retrieval
system, or transmitted, in any form or by any means—electronic,
mechanical, photocopying, recording, or otherwise—
without prior written permission.

For information:
MULTNOMAH BOOKS
12265 ORACLE BOULEVARD, SUITE 200
COLORADO SPRINGS, CO 80921
Library of Congress Cataloging-in-Publication Data
Harris, Joshua. Boy meets girl : say hello to courtship / by Joshua Harris.
p. cm. ISBN 1-59052-167-6
1-57673-709-8 (pbk.)
1. Single people—Religious life. 2. Courtship—Religious aspects—
Christianity. 3. Courtship. 4. Dating (Social customs)—Religious aspects—
Christianity. I. Title.

BV4596.S5 H36 2000 241'.6765–dc21 00-011254

09 10 — 25 24 23 22

To my bride, Shannon.
This book is the fruit of your
encouragement, humility, and sacrifice.
I love and cherish you.

———

Contents

Part 3: BEFORE YOU SAY "I DO"

AN INTRODUCTION

When I was single and twenty-one years old I wrote a book called *I Kissed Dating Goodbye*. It wasn't your typical book on relationships. It encouraged singles to be radically committed to honoring God in their relationships—even if it meant dumping the dating game. It was my own story of learning to trust God and wait on romance till I was ready for commitment.

To my astonishment, God provided a publisher willing to print my oddly titled book. To everyone's astonishment, the book actually sold. It turned out that many people besides me were rethinking romance. I have received thousands of e-mails, postcards, and letters from singles of all ages from all over the world who wanted to share their stories, ask questions, and get advice.

As the letters poured in, I realized that while God had graciously used my book to help some people, it had also raised a lot of questions. For example, if you don't date, how exactly do you end up married? One girl wrote: "I want to avoid the pitfalls of our culture's approach to romance, but how do I get close enough to a guy to decide whether I want to marry him? What comes between friendship and marriage?"

Boy Meets Girl is the answer to these questions—ones I

eventually had to wrestle with myself when I felt ready to pursue a girl with marriage in mind. It's a book about courtship, or what I like to call romance with purpose. It is filled with stories of ordinary people who are choosing to honor God in the real-life details of their love lives—from the agonizing questions about the timing of a relationship, to challenges like communicating well and remaining sexually pure when you're deeply in love.

Here's what you'll find in the book's three sections.

Part One defines the basic principles of courtship. We'll see how when we allow wisdom to guide our intense romantic feelings, our relationships are blessed by patience, purpose, and a clear grasp of reality. One couple's story will help us realize when we're ready to start a relationship and with whom, and we'll see how God intends to use this process to make us more like Him.

Part Two jumps into the practical issues of what to do as the season of courtship unfolds. We'll learn how to grow closer, but still guard our hearts in important areas like friendship, communication, fellowship, and romance. We'll get specific about our roles as men and women. We'll look at the importance of community during this time. Then we'll talk honestly about sexual purity and how we can prepare for a great sex life in marriage.

Part Three helps couples who are getting more serious to move toward marriage in a God-honoring way. We'll see how God's grace can help us face sin from our past. We'll ask some tough questions before engagement, including the all-important one: "Should we go forward together into marriage, or should we call our courtship off?" Finally, we'll be reminded that God's grace is our ultimate source of confidence for joining our hearts and lives in the vows of marriage.

As an added feature, you'll find a section at the back of the book called "Courtship Conversations: Eight Great Dates," developed with the help of my editors and friends, David and Heather Kopp. Our purpose has been to suggest activities and conversations that will help you get to know each other better, consider a possible future together, honor God in your relationship, and have plenty of fun.

Whether you're currently single, casually seeing someone, or in a serious relationship, I hope you'll take the time to read and wrestle with the ideas in this book. There's a good chance they will stretch your thinking and challenge your assumptions in healthy ways.

If you are in a relationship, I encourage you to read this book as a couple. Many have used this book to help understand how to grow their relationship and to set a clear course for deeper commitment.

As a single man, I wrote *I Kissed Dating Goodbye* to challenge the world's approach to romance. Today, as a married man, I write *Boy Meets Girl* to celebrate God's way in romance. I've seen just how good it is. And I want you to know that as you entrust your dreams of finding true love to His care, you will too.

part 1

RETHINKING
ROMANCE

Chapter One

WHAT I'VE LEARNED SINCE I KISSED DATING GOODBYE

From Waiting to Knowing— A Personal Story

The clock read 5:05 P.M. Shannon's workday was over. She enjoyed her job at the church, but she was ready to go home and unwind.

She began her familiar end-of-the-day routine: tidied her desk, shut down her computer, straightened a picture on her bookshelf, got her coat from the closet, and said her good-byes. "Bye, Nicole," she said to the girl in the office beside her. "See you tomorrow, Helen," she called to the receptionist.

She walked through the quiet lobby and pushed open one of the heavy glass doors. The winter wind tugged at her as she made her way across the nearly empty parking lot. She climbed into her worn, navy blue Honda Accord and shut out the cold.

She lifted her keys to the ignition, and then paused. There, alone in the silence, the emotions she had kept at bay during the day came rushing in. Tears welled up in her eyes. She leaned her forehead against the steering wheel and began to cry.

"Why, Lord?" she whispered. "Why is this so hard? What am I supposed to do with these feelings? Take them away if they're not from You."

I used to watch from my window as Shannon walked to her car at the end of each day. My office looked out over the parking lot. *What is she thinking about?* I wondered. I longed to know more about her—to go beyond our polite conversations as casual friends and coworkers and really get to know her.

But was it the right time? My heart had been wrong so many times before. Could I trust my feelings? Would she return my interest?

From my vantage point, Shannon Hendrickson seemed happy, confident, and oblivious of me. I was sure she liked another guy. As I watched her drive away, I whispered my own prayer. *What is Your will, God? Is she the one? Help me be patient. Show me when to act. Help me trust You.*

How could I know that the girl in the navy blue Honda was crying as she drove away, or that I was the cause of her tears?

Three months later. There I was, a twenty-three-year old, but my hands were acting like they'd never dialed a phone number. I gripped my cordless phone as if it were a wild animal trying to escape and tried again.

You can do this, I assured myself.

The phone rang three times before an answering machine picked up. She wasn't home. I gritted my teeth. *Should I leave a message?* The machine beeped, and I took the plunge.

"Hey, Shannon, this is Josh...uh, Harris."

I was sure my voice made it obvious how nervous I felt. I'd never called her at home before, and I had no excuse related to work or church for doing so now. "Um...could you give me a call when you get a chance? Thanks." I hung up, feeling like a complete idiot.

For sixty-four agonizing minutes I analyzed whether or not the message I had left sounded cool and collected. Then the phone rang. I took a deep breath and answered.

It was Shannon.

"Hey, thanks for calling me back. How's it going?"

We chatted for a few minutes about her day and did our best to have a natural conversation, even though we both knew that my calling her was the most unnatural thing in the world. I finally got to the point and asked if she could meet me the next day after work at Einstein's, a local bagel shop. She said she could.

Before we hung up, I offered an ambiguous explanation for the rendezvous. "I need to talk...about a guy I know who's interested in you."

A Change of Perspective

My phone call to Shannon might not seem like a big deal to most people, but for me it was monumental.

Why? Because I had quit dating. I know that sounds strange, so let me explain. I had come to believe that the lifestyle of recreational romance was a detour from serving God as a single. So while I kept my social life, my female friends, and my desire to get married someday, I stopped dating.

This new perspective was anything but characteristic of me.

I had always been a flirt who lived for the thrill of romance. For me, rejecting the dating game was a seismic shift.

My change of perspective began after I broke up with a girl I'd been going out with for two years. Our relationship was an area of my life that I had refused to submit to God. When it ended, He began to show me just how selfish I was. I'd used her to satisfy my own sinful desires. Even though we never went all the way, I'd led her into a sinful physical relationship. I had hurt her. I had broken a lot of promises.

For the first time, I really began to question how my faith as a Christian affected my love life. There had to be more to it than "don't have sex" and "only date Christians." What did it mean to truly love a girl? What did it feel like to really be pure—in my body *and* my heart? And how did God want me to spend my single years? Was it merely a time to try out different girls romantically?

Slowly and in spite of my resistance, God peeled away layer after layer of wrong thinking, wrong values, and wrong desires. He changed my heart. And as my heart changed, I saw that my lifestyle had to change too.

I wrote about my experience in my first book, *I Kissed Dating Goodbye*. I wanted to challenge other singles to reconsider the way they pursued a romance in light of God's Word. "If we aren't really ready for commitment, what's the point of getting into intimate and romantic relationships?" I asked. "Why not enjoy friendship with the opposite sex but use our energy as singles to serve God?"

The main point of *I Kissed Dating Goodbye* was: "If you're not ready for marriage, *wait* on romance."

But now, five years later, I was asking the question, "How can you know when you *are* ready for marriage? And once you're ready, what should you do?"

This is why my phone call to Shannon was such a big deal. I'd reached a point where I felt I *was* ready to pursue marriage, and I was deeply attracted to her. What now? I had experienced God's faithfulness as I *waited* on romance; now I was stepping into the unknown believing that He would continue to be faithful as I *pursued* romance.

The guy who had "kissed dating goodbye" was about to "say hello to courtship."

The next evening I arrived early for my meeting with Shannon. Einstein's Bagels is a favorite lunch spot in Gaithersburg, but in the evenings it's all but empty. I chose a lonely table in a back corner of the restaurant. It was slightly dirty, so I asked the server to wipe it off. Everything needed to be just right. I went to the bathroom and checked my hair. "Oh, whatever," I finally said to the mirror.

Back at the table I waited and fidgeted in my seat. I worried about whether I should prop my feet up on a chair. Would it make me look more relaxed? No, it's too casual. How about one foot? No, that looks like I'm wounded. I finally decided to leave both feet on the floor.

Nervous energy washed over me every time I thought about the conversation I was about to have. I couldn't believe that I was doing this—that in only a few minutes she would be sitting across from me.

Shannon's Awakening

Shannon Hendrickson and I had been friends for about a year. We worked in the same office. She was a secretary and I was an intern. The first thing I noticed about Shannon was her eyes—they were a bluish, greenish, gray color, and they sparkled when she smiled. The second thing was how tiny she was. Exactly five feet tall, Shannon defines the word *petite*. I liked that. Since I was only five foot six myself, a girl who actually looked up into my eyes was a rare find.

I caught my first glimpse of her on the Sunday she got up in church and shared the story of how she'd become a Christian. Two and a half years earlier she'd had no interest in God. At the time she'd just returned to Maryland from college in New Hampshire, where she'd lived the typical party life. It was an empty life lived for herself—a life ruled by sin. Back home, she threw all her energy into her dream of becoming a professional singer. Soon a move to Nashville seemed the next sensible step up the ladder of stardom. That's just the kind of person she was. Her parents had gotten divorced when she was nine, and her dad had raised her to be self-reliant. She would set her sights on a goal, and then do whatever was needed to get there.

Before heading to Nashville, she wanted to take a few guitar lessons. She asked around about a teacher, and a friend referred her to a guitarist named Brian, who was looking for students. What Shannon didn't know was that Brian was a Christian and was looking for opportunities to share his faith. Her guitar lessons would turn out to be soul saving.

After a few weeks of lessons, Brian told Shannon how Jesus had changed his life. She listened politely but said she could never live like he did. "I respect you, but that's not for me."

"Do you think you're going to heaven?" Brian asked gently.

"I think I'm basically a good person," she responded.

But her confident rejection was an act. She couldn't get Brian's questions out of her head. What if there was a God? If He existed, would she be willing to live for Him?

Shannon secretly began to study Christianity. She read the book of Romans, which described her not as a "good person," but as a sinner in need of a Savior. She visited a Christian bookstore and asked for something that would help a person explore the claims of Christianity. "It's for a friend," she explained. She left with Josh McDowell's *More Than a Carpenter,* which gave historical proof for Christ's life, death, and resurrection.

God was drawing Shannon. He was whittling away at her pride and independence and awakening within her a longing for Himself. One night, alone in her room, she repented for her sinful and self-centered life and believed on the Savior she now knew had died for her.

Something Better

Growing up, I always hoped that when I saw the girl I was going to marry, it would be love at first sight. As it turned out, my chance for a "love at first sight" moment went right over my head.

On the Sunday I heard Shannon tell her story, I happened to be interested in a girl named Rachel. In fact, I was sitting next to Rachel's mother that morning. When Shannon finished speaking, Rachel's mom leaned over and noted what a "cute girl" Shannon was, a remark that I now find very ironic.

God had set me up.

As I sat there next to the mother of *my* plan for my future, God was parading *His* plan for my future right in front of my eyes. He had mapped a course for me that was more wonderful than anything I could come up with on my own, and He was making sure that in the days to come I would never question that this good plan had originated in *His* mind.

Three months later Shannon and I wound up working together at the church office. We hit it off right away, but I wasn't thinking about anything beyond friendship. When someone asked me if I was interested in her, I thought the question was silly. Shannon was a terrific girl, I said, but not the kind of person I envisioned marrying. Besides, our backgrounds were too different. She was a new Christian from a broken home. I'd probably marry someone who had been homeschooled and raised in the church like I had—someone like Rachel.

But over the next six months my plans for a future with Rachel began to unravel like a cheap sweater. I remember the afternoon I found out that she liked another guy. Rachel and I had only been friends, and she hadn't led me on, but it still hurt. I needed to talk to God. I shut my office door; but that didn't seem private enough, so I squeezed myself into my small office closet and pulled the door shut.

There in the darkness I started to cry. I wasn't mad at Rachel; I wasn't bitter. I cried because I knew God was behind it all. He was the one who had closed the door on a relationship with Rachel, and He'd done it for my good. I was overwhelmed by the thought that the God of the universe was willing to be involved in the details of my life—that He'd be willing to reach down and shut a door that He didn't want me to walk through.

Still crying, I began to thank Him. "I don't understand, but I thank You," I said. "I don't understand, but I know You are good. I don't understand, but I know You're taking this away because You have something better."

That day was a turning point. I stopped trusting in my own carefully laid plans and asked God to show me His.

Change of Heart

Around that time I began to see Shannon in a new light. Her kindness to others and me caught my attention. She had a passion for God and a maturity that belied her short time as a believer. How can I explain it? She just began to pop up in my thoughts and prayers. I looked forward to the chance to see her and talk. What I learned about her through our interaction and from what I heard from others impressed me. I saw that all the reasons I had for why I wouldn't be interested in her were shallow. God was changing my heart.

All this had made the months leading up to my phone call torturous. I went through the "I shouldn't be distracted by this" phase. Then the "I *am* distracted by this" phase. And finally, the "I'm going to fight this" phase, in which I swore to stop journaling about her and mapped a new course around the office so that I wouldn't walk past her desk ten times every hour—something I found myself doing "unintentionally."

I was living with my pastor, C. J., at the time. Since my mom and dad lived far away in Oregon, C. J. and his wife, Carolyn, had become like a second set of parents to me. I told them about my interest in Shannon. Their counsel helped keep me on track: "Don't let impatience get the upper hand. Be her friend, but don't communicate your interest until you're ready to start a relationship that has a clear purpose and direction. You don't want to play with her heart."

It wasn't easy. I would swing between the conviction that I needed to conceal my feelings and the urge to send her signals just to find out if there was any mutual interest. I could trust God better if I knew she liked me, I argued. But deep down I knew this wasn't true. I needed to be a man—a noncommittal testing of the waters wouldn't be fair to her.

I started seeking the advice of the most trusted people in my life—my parents, my pastor, and people from our church who knew Shannon and me well. Was I prepared spiritually and emotionally for marriage? Could I provide for a wife and family? Was this God's time for me to pursue a relationship? My prayers kicked into high gear.

Instead of subsiding, my feelings grew. My circle of counselors gave me nothing but encouragement to pursue a relationship. I didn't know if Shannon and I were supposed to be married, but I felt that God was directing me to take the next step.

Corner Table

The corner table at Einstein's was it. The countless prayers and conversations had led to this moment. After months of keeping my feelings hidden from Shannon, I was about to make them known.

Shannon walked through the door right on time. She seemed calm. I walked to the front to greet her, and then we got in line to order something. I looked up at the menu on the wall and acted like I was studying it, but food was the furthest thing from my mind.

"Are you hungry?" I asked her.

"No, not really."

"Yeah, me neither. Something to drink?"

"Sure."

We both ordered Sprites and sat down.

Now there was no delaying the inevitable. I needed to say what I had come to say.

"You may have already figured this out," I began. "That guy I wanted to talk to you about—you know, the one who's interested in you? Well...it's me."

———

Chapter Two

REDISCOVERING COURTSHIP

A Return to Purposeful Romance

A bagel shop isn't the most romantic spot to tell a girl you like her. But on that specific night, romance wasn't the priority. Our time there wasn't intended to be mushy. I didn't propose marriage or say I was madly in love with her, and she didn't swoon.

What I did tell her was that through our friendship I'd grown to respect her. I couldn't know at that point if we were right for each other, but I wanted to find out. I asked her to take a step with me into courtship, a new season of friendship. The purpose of this time would be to deepen our relationship so that we could prayerfully and purposefully explore the possibility of marriage.

Actually, I didn't say it that well. I stammered, laughed nervously, and was anything but eloquent. In fact, I forgot to use the term *courtship*. She had to ask me if that's what I meant.

Ultimately, it wasn't the word itself that mattered. What did matter, I told her, was that our relationship have a clearly defined direction. I didn't want to play games with her. Although I wanted us to start going on dates, I wasn't interested in dating for the sake of dating. I wanted more than anything else to please God and find out if marriage was *His* plan for us. And I wanted this process to be one we could look back on with fondness and without regret—whether or not we married each other.

"You don't have to give me an answer tonight," I told her. "You can take as long as you need to think about it." Then I shut up.

Shannon didn't say anything for a moment. She looked down at her Sprite and played with her straw.

"Well," she finally said, "I could torture you by dragging it out and leaving you hanging. You know, being 'mysterious.' But I can tell you now that I'm willing to give it a try. I don't want you to get the impression that I'm taking this lightly or think that I don't need to pray about it…" She paused. "It's just that I *have* been praying about this."

She'd been praying about me? She'd been *thinking* about me? I wanted to jump up and tear around the restaurant screaming. Instead I just nodded my head and said, "That's wonderful."

What *Is* Courtship?

If all this sounds strange to you, I understand. The first time I heard about courtship, it sounded like a bunch of silly rules from the horse-and-buggy days. But the irony is that while the word may sound old-fashioned, the principles of courtship are anything but. In fact, as you'll see, those principles are desperately needed in relationships today.

Think about the questions Christian singles wrestle with: How do you get close enough to someone to make a decision about marriage without stealing the privileges of marriage? How do you find the love of your life without leaving a trail of broken hearts and broken promises behind you on the way to the altar?

This is where "old-fashioned" courtship begins to make a lot of sense.

Throughout history, communities and couples knew that meaningful intimacy shouldn't outpace commitment. So they adopted certain practices—certain agreed-upon guidelines for behavior—that helped them balance appropriate intimacy with the level of commitment. A man only pursued a woman romantically when he had the intention of pursuing marriage. He honored the protective care of the girl's parents by seeking their approval for pursuing their daughter. With intentions clearly understood a couple was given the privileges of time together. A physical relationship was saved for the total commitment of marriage.

While the word *courtship* isn't in the Bible, the principles that comprise courtship are timeless and, I believe, rooted in God's word. In God's plan the personal benefits of an intimate relationship—emotional or sexual—are always inseparably linked to a commitment to the other person's long-term good inside the covenant of marriage. To put it simply, the joy of intimacy is the reward of commitment. Courtship is simply a relationship guided by this principle.

Courtship is a relationship between a man and a woman who are actively and intentionally together to consider marriage. And it draws on principles we'll look at in coming chapters about how to genuinely love others, the priority of sexual purity, and our need for the wisdom and perspective that comes from community.

You might not like the term *courtship*. That's okay. There's nothing sacred about it. Ultimately the term we use for relationships doesn't matter as much as how we live.

Relationships on Purpose

That night in the bagel shop was the beginning of an amazing journey for me and Shannon—it wasn't always easy and we had to learn to depend on God together. But for us the season of courtship was a wonderful time in our relationship in which we refrained from physical intimacy, deepened our friendship, learned about each other's values and goals, and interacted on a spiritual level. We asked a lot of questions. We went on dates. We grew closer to each other and ultimately grew to love one another deeply. The key was that everything we did in our relationship *was for the very clearly stated purpose of finding out if God would have us marry.*

And that's really the essential element of courtship—it's doing a relationship on purpose.

Some people ask why I bothered to initiate a defined season of courtship with Shannon. Why not just ask her out and see where it went? I did it because I didn't want another undefined romantic relationship. Too many times in the past

I had separated the pursuit of intimacy from the responsibility of commitment. I had learned that this was neither a wise nor caring way to treat a girl.

When I expressed my desire to explore the possibility of marriage, I wanted to set a clear course for our relationship—a course that would lead to marriage if it was truly God's will.

Unlike my past relationships, my courtship with Shannon was unambiguous. From the start, our pursuit of intimacy was paired with an openness to commitment. The difference was that now our activities and the time we spent together had a purpose beyond mere recreation, and that purpose was clearly defined.

Do you see the difference? We were walking toward the commitment of marriage, not simply seeing how romantically involved we could become for the sake of a good time. Were the feelings there? You bet! Our courtship was an unforgettable time of growing to love each other passionately. But we weren't simply trying to get swept up in our emotions. Instead, we were letting our feelings grow naturally out of our deepening respect, friendship, and commitment to one another. Setting a clear course for a defined season of courtship helped us keep from rushing into involvement with our hearts and bodies before we had time to get to know each other's mind and character.

Why So Serious?

I know that for some people using the term *courtship* or mentioning the possibility of marriage feels like too much pressure, too soon. For these people it's important to note that even though courtship has a serious intent, it can be low-pressure and casual when it begins.

Think of courtship as a pathway that leads into deepening levels of seriousness as it progresses. The path starts with "I'd like to get to know you" and ends—if the outcome is a desire for a life together—with "I'd like to marry you." But there's a lot of space in between. If you're in the just-getting-to-know-each-other phase, you can make that clear to the person you're courting as well as to others who know about your relationship.

We shouldn't make courtship a bigger deal than it really is. When someone tells me they're in a courtship, I don't say, "Congratulations!" as if they got engaged. That's not what the initial stages of courtship are about. It's a time for the couple to get to know each other without outside pressure or overly high expectations.

The only pressure a couple should feel when they begin a courtship is the good pressure God's Word places on them to honor Him and treat each other with purity and integrity. It's this desire that can keep us from making courtship just dating with a different name.

So even though courtship shouldn't be too serious, too soon, it shouldn't be embarked on lightly either. In one sense, courtship is a commitment—it's a promise not to play games with another person's heart. In that sense it's serious. It's a willingness to honestly explore the merits of a lifelong commitment. The man is setting a clear course for the romance by answering the "What's the point?" question about the relationship at the very outset. The point of the relationship will be to consider marriage.

Different Students, One Master

I've shared a little of the Joshua-meets-Shannon story with you. And in the following chapters I'll introduce you to other couples who have sought to apply the principles of courtship in their relationship. But as you keep reading, remember that God doesn't have a one-size-fits-all plan for relationships.

We all have very different lives—we vary in age, cultural background, and circumstances, to name just a few. Some of us can have our parents involved in our courtships; others cannot. Some of us can develop a friendship with another person naturally in a group setting at church or school. Others don't have the luxury of those settings and have to be more obvious about their interest. Some of us approach the possibility of marriage for the first time, while others have journeyed through the nightmare of divorce and are hesitantly moving toward a second commitment.

You might be asking, "How am I supposed to follow God's principles for courtship when my circumstances are so different from those of other people?" Let me try to explain.

Imagine that you're a student in an art class. You and dozens of classmates are learning from a master painter. One day your teacher displays a painting of his own. It's an incredible work of art, and he wants each of you to copy it.

You're about to begin working when you turn to look at the person next to you. You're surprised to note that he has a larger brush than you and a different kind of canvas. You look around at the rest of the class. Some students have acrylic paint, others watercolor, still others oil—and everyone is using different colors. Though you all have the same assignment, you each have completely different materials. This frustrates you. Some students have materials you would prefer for yourself. Why should they get them?

You're not the only student to notice the disparity. A hand goes up on your left. A girl with only a ragged brush and three pale shades of blue on her palette is noticeably agitated. "This isn't fair," she tells the teacher. "How do you expect me to duplicate your painting when the people around me have so many more colors to choose from?"

The teacher smiles. "Don't worry about the other students," he says. "I've carefully chosen brushes and paints for each of you. Trust me. You have what you need to complete the assignment. Remember, your goal is not to create a painting that mirrors the person next to you, but to do your best with the materials I've given you to replicate *my* painting."

This is our assignment in courtship. It's good to be inspired by couples who have set a godly example. Still, God isn't asking us to copy each other but to fix our eyes on our Lord and Master Jesus Christ and pursue courtship in a way that's faithful to His character. We can each rest in the knowledge that God is sovereign over our life's situation. No matter where we are today or what mistakes we've made in the past, He has given us everything we need to glorify Him right now.

Courtship Movement?

A newspaper reporter once asked me to comment on the "courtship movement" and the implications of this old-fashioned way of approaching relationships making a comeback. I didn't have much to say. I've never wanted to be part of a courtship movement. The goal of doing courtship shouldn't be to feel morally superior or to achieve a heartache-proof relationship or to join some courtship coalition. The motivating purpose of Christians should be to obey God. The concept of courtship is only helpful so far as it helps us to better honor and glorify God. That should be the ultimate purpose in any relationship.

So, yes, I do hope to convince you that courtship is a better approach to romance. But ultimately it's not courtship that I want to point you toward. The aim of this book is to help you place God squarely in the middle of your love life—to show that the journey from friendship to matrimony, from "How do you do?" to "I do," should be viewed as an opportunity both to revel in the joys of love and to enjoy, honor, and glorify the *Creator* of love. Making Him our greatest delight and joy is the best thing we can do for our relationships and future marriages. The simple, biblical principles this book contains can help you do that and can guide you to the deeply romantic and committed relationship for which you've been praying.

So what is courtship? Basically it's a really good idea…and not as strange as you might first think. It's dating with a purpose. It's romance chaperoned by wisdom. It's a way of approaching relationships that can help us live out the truths of God's Word as we pursue our heart's desire. It's a story of boy meets girl, where—whether you choose to marry or not—you can get to know each other in the confidence that you have only God's very best ahead for each of you.

ROMANCE AND WISDOM: A MATCH MADE IN HEAVEN

Why You Need More than Just Intense Feelings

This spot will do, Rich thought sadly. He peered over his shoulder into the darkness to make sure no one was watching, then raised his shovel and drove it into the earth.

Clang!

The sound of steel hitting rock rang out in the stillness of the night. He dropped to the ground, his heart pounding. *Good grief!* At this rate he'd rouse the whole neighborhood. He clenched his teeth at the thought of waking someone inside Christy's house. What if her dad came out to investigate and discovered him? What explanation could he possibly give his ex-girlfriend's father for being in his front yard with a shovel at 3 A.M.? He tried not to think about it.

Rich held his breath and waited. A minute passed, and

no one in the house stirred. All was quiet. Slowly he stood up and resumed his work, this time with greater care. The noise of his digging still seemed unbearably loud, but he decided to keep at it. Christy and her family lived in the Virginia countryside and had a big front yard. Rich was probably a hundred yards from the house. They'd never hear him. At least he hoped they wouldn't....

The Amazing Gift of Romance

Before I explain why Rich Shipe was digging a hole in Christy Farris's front yard, I need to back up a little. This is quite a story—in fact, it's one of the most romantic I've ever heard. But that's not my only reason for sharing it. This story will do more than merely warm your heart. It's an inspiring example of what happens when romance—and all those feelings of passion, excitement, and urgency that go with it—is guided by wisdom. And that's what this chapter is all about.

Four years before his secret excavation in her front yard, Rich had met Christy at the small Bible church they both attended. They were fourteen years old. Rich thought Christy was really cute; Christy thought Rich was really annoying. Fortunately for Rich, he didn't stay fourteen. And as time passed, he and Christy became good friends. During their senior year of high school, their relationship became romantic. They began to write each other—not e-mail, mind you, but old-fashioned, handwritten letters—to express their feelings. Each letter was written from the heart with love.

Falling in love wasn't something Rich and Christy could easily explain. Who among us can describe the mysterious and powerful urge to pursue another person's affection? Words just don't do it justice. Defining romance is like trying to capture the grandeur of the Grand Canyon with a disposable camera. No matter how many snapshots you take, your attempts fall short.

And guess what? Falling in love was God's idea. He was the one who made us capable of experiencing romantic feelings. He was the one who gave us the ability to appreciate beauty and experience attraction. And He was the one who invented marriage so that the blazing fire of romantic love could become something even more beautiful—a pulsing, red-hot ember of covenant love in marriage.

Why did He do it? For the same reason that He made sunsets and mountain ranges and fireflies! Because He's good. Because He wants to give us a million different opportunities to see just how wonderful He is.

Think about the first man and woman God created. The story of Adam and Eve is the original "boy meets girl." Their love story shows so clearly that God is the Author of romance. Though we don't usually think of Adam and Eve's story as a love story, it is bursting with romance. They were humans like you and me. They saw, they felt, they desired. Can you imagine the moment their eyes first met? Picture it. What would it be like to behold a beautiful member of the opposite sex when you had never known or imagined an opposite sex existed?

Sparks flew.

There was chemistry between those two like nothing you've ever seen. And here's the most incredible part: God was watching and rejoicing over it all. He was the one who arranged the original match. God, who spoke galaxies into existence, was finding joy in the beauty of romance between a man and a woman. I can't help thinking that God was smiling as He watched the hearts of the first two humans beating faster than ever before.

Until Love So Desires

Romance is a very good thing. But just because it's good doesn't mean that we can enjoy it whenever and however we please. Like all the other good gifts God has made, romantic love can be misused.

Even the Song of Solomon, which revels in the ecstasy of romantic passion, is filled with reminders not to remove that passion from the boundaries of God's timing and purpose. "I charge you," Solomon's bride says, "do not arouse or awaken love until it so desires" (Song of Solomon 8:4).

Rich and Christy's feelings for each other were real and deeply romantic. But were those feelings being awakened in God's timing and purpose? Christy's dad, Mike Farris, wasn't so sure. When he found out how emotionally involved Rich and Christy were, he decided to intervene.

Mike had the chance to interact with Rich on a regular basis—he was his boss. Mike was running for the office of lieutenant governor in Virginia and had hired Rich to drive him to the different rallies and events being held around the state. On most of these trips, Mike worked quietly in the backseat or made phone calls. But to Rich's surprise, one day Mike decided to sit up front. As soon as they were under way, Mike turned to Rich and asked, "So what's this I hear about you and Christy?"

Rich gulped.

As Rich drove, Mike talked to him gently and with fatherly concern about the importance of wisdom in romance. Mike had many regrets about the years he had spent dating girls in high school and college. "When you're close emotionally, you give away part of your heart," he told Rich. "There are long-term consequences."

To his credit, Rich really listened to what Mike had to say.

The truth sank in. Rich wasn't ready to support a family—both he and Christy still wanted to attend college. And it was also too soon for them to stoke the fires of romance. A premature romantic relationship would only distract them from preparing for their future.

"I had never heard anything like that before," Rich remembers. "Mike convinced me. It wasn't a case of him forcing me to break up with his daughter. As he shared his own understanding about relationships, I saw that he was right."

Three Words

Ending what he and Christy called the "us" part of their relationship wasn't easy, but they both knew it needed to happen. They went back to being just friends. They interacted at church but didn't act like a couple. They thought of each other as brother and sister, not boyfriend and girlfriend.

The plan worked…for a while. Even though they both knew what was right, their hearts were deceitful. They *wanted* the feelings. They *wanted* the thrill of expressing how they felt. They *wanted* the security of knowing they belonged to each other. As a result they began to compromise their commitment to keep the relationship strictly a friendship. In a letter, Rich told Christy that he loved her. She did the same. They did nothing physically, but before they knew it, they were back in a full-throttle romantic relationship, this time behind her father's back.

But after several months, conviction set in. Deceiving Christy's parents began to take its toll on them. "We have to tell your parents," Rich told Christy one day. "We can't go on like this."

They never got the chance. A day later, Christy's dad walked by while she was on the phone talking with a girl-friend about her relationship with Rich.

"Christy, what were you talking about?" her dad asked when she had hung up. "Tell me in three words."

"Personal prayer requests," Christy answered.

"Really?" her dad asked. "It sounded more like, 'Richard Guy Shipe.'"

They were caught.

Christy broke down and confessed her deceit. Rich met with Christy's parents a few days later. Like Christy, he was brokenhearted at the way he had deceived them. He'd gone back on his word to Mike. He'd stolen more of Christy's affections when he knew they didn't rightfully belong to him.

Rich asked Mike and his wife, Vickie, for forgiveness. This time, he promised, the relationship really was going to end. He understood now that this would require drastic measures. They couldn't simply be casual friends. "If we didn't pull back, we would be moving forward," Rich says. "You can't stand still in a relationship like that." They had to get out of each other's lives.

That's when Rich asked Christy to give back all the letters he had ever written her. Reluctantly she handed them over. "I wanted to serve her," Rich explains. "I wanted to take everything from her that represented my feelings for her. Those letters were the record of our love and all we had shared. We cherished them and reread them over and over. I knew that in order to truly lay the relationship down at God's feet, we both had to part with them."

An Early Morning Funeral

Rich was digging a hole in Christy's front yard that night to bury a box that contained all the letters they'd written each other. There were over one hundred handwritten pages inside it.

Had his feelings for Christy changed? Not at all. But he realized that he couldn't be guided just by his feelings. He had to act on principle and do what was in Christy's best interest. He couldn't just do what *felt* right; he had to do what *was* right. Even though it hurt, he knew that the most caring thing he could do for the girl he loved was to get out of her life and end the relationship that was distracting both of them from serving God and obeying her parents.

It took Rich nearly two hours of digging to finish the hole. He made it two feet wide by three feet long and eighteen inches deep so it would be beneath the frost line. He picked up the box of letters and laid it gently into the ground. He had wrapped it tightly in several layers of plastic. Rich wanted his hopes to be able to stay in the ground for a long time…maybe even forever.

For eighteen-year-old Rich, that moment was the funeral of his dreams. He was submitting his feelings and longings to God. He stared at the box one last time, looked up at the quiet house, and then pushed the dirt he'd unearthed back into the hole and packed it down with his foot. *If You want to dig this up someday, I know You can,* he told God. *But if not, this is where it will stay.*

He covered the spot with sod, then quietly stole away.

The Kite and the String

I don't want you to get the wrong idea from Rich and Christy's story. Matching romance with wisdom doesn't necessarily mean that you do the opposite of what you want. What it does mean is that you learn to do what's best. Wisdom is simply the ownership of insight. It's the "Oh, I get it!" that means we understand how one thing relates to another...and that we're willing to change our attitudes and behavior accordingly.

I like the way Eugene Peterson describes wisdom. He says that it's "the art of living skillfully in whatever actual conditions we find ourselves." When we guide romance with wisdom, we have *skillful* romance—romance that is directed by what is true about God and about the world He has made.

I like to think that the relationship between wisdom and romance is like the one between a string and a kite. Romantic love is the kite that catches the wind and tenaciously heads for the sky; wisdom is the string that tugs downward, holding it back. The tension is real, but healthy.

I suppose there are times when a kite feels tied down by

the string. "If this bothersome string would just let go of me, I could fly really high," the kite might think. But that isn't true, is it? Without the string holding it in the face of the wind, the kite would quickly come crashing to the ground.

In the same way, romance without wisdom will soon take a nosedive. It becomes selfish, indulgent, and even idolatrous. Have you been in a relationship like this? Have you witnessed such a relationship in the life of a friend? What was it missing? The answer is wisdom.

It's not enough to simply *have* romantic feelings. Anyone can do that! Long-lasting romance needs practical, common-sense wisdom that knows when to let the wind of feelings carry us higher and when to pull back. When to express our emotions and when to keep quiet. When to open our hearts and when to rein them in.

The Art of Skillful Romance

Let me share some practical examples of what I mean. The following are three ways that wisdom leads and guides us into skillful romantic relationships.

1. Romance says, "I want it now!" Wisdom urges patience.

Proverbs 19:11 says, "A man's wisdom gives him patience." My biggest mistakes in romantic relationships were almost all the result of impatience. Is this true in your life?

Like Rich and Christy, maybe you just couldn't wait to express your feelings for someone and wound up starting a relationship prematurely. Or maybe you got impatient waiting for God to bring someone godly into your life, so you got involved with someone you shouldn't have. You couldn't regret it more.

It takes patience to wait to start a relationship until you're truly ready to court with purpose. Then after you've started a purposeful relationship, you'll need patience to make sure it unfolds at a *healthy pace*. Impatience rushes everything. It urges us to skip the time and attention a healthy friendship requires and to jump right into emotional and physical intimacy.

On Julia's first date with Matt, she dove headfirst into an emotionally intimate relationship. They had gone out to dinner and afterwards stopped at Bibo's Juice for fruit smoothies. Not being the shy type, Matt confessed that he was attracted to Julia. She admitted that the feeling was mutual.

What followed that flirtatious exchange was a marathon tour of each other's personal lives. Impatience put them on the fast track. "We just instantly connected," Julia remembers. Everything came out in that first conversation. She poured out her life, telling him about her struggles as a new Christian and about mistakes with ex-boyfriends—preconversion and postconversion. "I told him parts of my testimony that are very personal," Julia says. Matt did the same. Though they had known each other only a brief time, their conversation instantly threw their relationship into high gear. They felt close, even though they hadn't taken the time to nurture a friendship or get a reality check on each other's character.

In the months that followed they continued to be driven

by impatience. They felt close, but they wanted more. The rush of romance was intoxicating; but eventually, as with all highs, the fervor leveled off—illusion gave way to reality. Although Matt had told her that he had left his old life behind, Julia discovered that he was still living sinfully and secretly partying. Their relationship ended bitterly. Today Julia deeply regrets that she shared so much of her heart with Matt.

Mishmash Romance

Just because a couple is at a place in their lives where they can seriously consider marriage doesn't mean that they should proceed recklessly. I call a relationship like Julia and Matt's "mishmash romance." It makes me think of going out to a fine restaurant with someone who doesn't have the patience to wait for each course of the meal to be served. The master chef has a wonderful plan that takes time to appreciate fully. But instead of enjoying each course individually, your date insists that all the courses—the drinks, the soup, the salad, the entrée, the dessert—be blended together into one bowl of mishmash. Yuck!

Imagine sucking that slop through a straw, and you've got a good picture of what many relationships are like today. Instead of savoring the "courses" of an unfolding love story—acquaintance, friendship, courtship, engagement, marriage—impatient couples mash the sequence together. Before they've built a friendship, they start playing at love. Before they've even thought about commitment, they're acting as though they own each other. Mishmash romance, like mishmash food, is an unappetizing mess.

Wisdom calls us to slow down. We can be patient because

we know that God is sovereign and that He is faithful. "I wait for you, O LORD; you will answer, O LORD my God" (Psalm 38:15). Patience is an expression of trust that God, the Master Chef, can serve up an exquisite relationship. This lets us enjoy each part of our love story. We can be faithful and content right where we are—whether it's in friendship or courtship or engagement—and not try to steal the privileges God has reserved for a later season.

My dad likes to say that time is God's way of keeping everything from happening all at once. If you're not ready to get married, don't grab at a relationship. Patiently wait for the right time to start one that can eventually lead to marriage. If you are ready for marriage and you're in a relationship, don't let impatience cause you to rush. Take your time. Enjoy where God has the two of you *right now.* Savor each course. Don't settle for mishmash.

2. Romance says, "This is what I want and it's good for me." Wisdom leads us to consider what's best for the other person.

In James 3:17 we're told, "The wisdom that comes from heaven is first of all pure; then peace-loving, considerate, submissive, full of mercy and good fruit, impartial and sincere." Add up all these qualities and you see that wisdom in relationships involves a selfless desire to do what's best for the other person. This important quality of a God-glorifying relationship is summed up in the Golden Rule: "Do to others as you would have them do to you" (Luke 6:31). It's simple, and yet it encompasses every facet of a relationship.

Sincere, Christlike love for the man or woman you're in a

relationship with is the natural outgrowth of love for God. The two are so closely intertwined that it's difficult to tell where one ends and the other begins—they weave in and out of each other. This is why when Jesus was asked to name the greatest commandment, He gave two—to love God and to love others. They can't be separated. When we serve others, we're serving our Lord (Matthew 25:40). Jesus laid His life down for us to show us what love is, and He calls us to follow His example (1 John 3:16). The Word tells us to humble ourselves, to consider others better than ourselves, and to look to their interests first (Philippians 2:3–4).

We glorify God in our relationships when we put our needs aside and base our decisions on what serves the interests of the other person. Listen to the kinds of questions we ask when we're guided by a selfless desire to do what's best for another:

- Is starting this relationship now what's best for him?
- Will expressing all my feelings now serve her?
- Are my actions encouraging him to love God more?
- Am I communicating clearly and in a way that helps her?
- Does the way I dress encourage him to have a pure thought life?
- Will kissing her be what's best for her in the long run?

A selfless desire to do what's best for the other person can guide us in the big and small decisions of a relationship. It's not tedious. It's an expression of sincere love and the defining mark of a Christian relationship. "By this all men will

know that you are my disciples, if you love one another"
(John 13:35).

3. Romance says, "Enjoy the fantasy." Wisdom calls us to base our emotions and perceptions in reality.

Proverbs 19:2 says, "It is not good to have zeal without knowledge, nor to be hasty and miss the way." That verse could stand as a one-line summary of Shakespeare's tragic play *Romeo and Juliet* and for many misguided romances in real life. To be passionate about something if our passion is based on ignorance or mistaken information invites disaster. Yet the very intensity of romance can set us up for exactly that.

Earlier I told you about Matt and Julia. They're an example of two people who, motivated by impatience and selfishness, became very emotionally zealous about each other but later realized that their emotions were based in fantasy. They didn't really know each other. Their emotions had no foundation in the facts.

What is an emotion? As I was growing up, my dad taught me that an emotion is a physical expression of how we perceive the status of something we value. Anger, gladness, fear, sadness, joy, jealousy, and hatred are all combinations of our *perception* and our *values*. For example, two bystanders who witness a cat being hit by a car can experience totally different emotions based on how they perceive the situation and how they value the cat. One who hates cats might be wickedly glad, while the other person who owns and loves the cat would be overcome with sadness.

In a relationship, if our values are godly and our perception of what we value is accurate, our emotions will be appropriate and healthy. But if either is out of sync with the truth, our emotions will be inappropriate and unhealthy. Our goal should be to be properly excited about what is really important.

Wisdom calls us to base feelings on accurate information, not on distortions. This is what Julia failed to do. Her emotions created an image of Matt that wasn't real. She rushed heart-first into the relationship with her eyes closed. Her marathon conversation with Matt on their first date created a false sense of knowledge. They revealed parts of themselves that were very intimate but didn't get the reality check of time or observe each other in different contexts. The effect was to give them the impression that they were closer than they really were.

In the season of courtship we have to fight the tendency to fill what's lacking in our knowledge of the other person with emotion based on fantasy. If we don't know something about him or her, we need to talk, ask probing questions, and discover who they really are—their values, their motivations, their goals. We need to move beyond typical, artificial dating activities and observe each other in real-life settings—in families, in church life, with friends, handling pressure at work. Courtship is a time to see the good, the bad, and the ugly in the one we love. Then our emotions and decisions about the relationship can be based on fact.

The skillful romance I've been talking about doesn't disdain or rule out emotions and passion. But it does call us to make sure that these feelings are flowing from reality, not wishful thinking or rationalization. We want the true character of someone to win our heart. We want our emotions to respond to who they really are and to the true status of the relationship.

Are You Ready for Courtship?

The problems we see in relationships today—the impatience, the lack of purpose, and the misguided emotions—are all expressions of foolishness. We need wisdom. Wisdom complements romance. Like the string attached to the kite, wisdom enables romance to really soar. It anchors it, disciplines it, and brings it to its highest potential. Again, the tension is good.

When the emotional winds get dangerously strong, wisdom pulls the kite down to safety so it won't be destroyed. That's what happened in Rich and Christy's story. Even though it was difficult, they grounded their romantic relationship because it wasn't the right time for it to fly.

I talk to many couples like Rich and Christy who ask, "How do we know when it's the right time to start a courtship?" The basic answer to the question is that *you're ready to start a courtship when you can match romance with wisdom*. Others couples are already in a relationship but they want to realign it with the principles of courtship. If you're already deeply involved, can you turn a relationship into a wisdom-guided courtship midway? Every situation is different, but it's definitely possible. What's important is that both the man and woman share the desire to submit themselves to godly wisdom. If only one person has this goal, trying to refocus the relationship doesn't usually work. Be willing to push the pause button on your relationship so you can prayerfully and honestly evaluate your readiness for wisdom-guided romance.

In fact, let's turn the three points we just looked at into questions to help you examine your own readiness for courtship.

Are you able to be patient? It's not wrong to desire marriage. But what would you say your greatest motive is for starting a relationship? Is it the confidence that you're ready for marriage and that God has brought someone godly into your life? Or is it impatience? Are you characterized by peace or anxiousness? Don't start a courtship until you can proceed patiently.

Can you set a clear course for the relationship? I remember having a thirteen-year-old kid stop me at a conference. He was holding his girlfriend's hand. "We stopped dating," he said proudly. "Now we're courting!" I smiled at his misguided concept of courtship. You can't have a purposeful relationship or set a clear course for it when marriage is so far off. The same guideline applies to a thirty-year-old who isn't really sure he wants to get married. If you're not willing for a relationship to succeed and progress to engagement and marriage in a reasonable period of time, you probably shouldn't be starting it.

Are your emotions based in reality? As we saw earlier, our emotions are the result of value and perception. First, do you have the right values about relationships? Maybe you just became a Christian or are just beginning to obey God in this part of your life. Don't rush into a relationship too quickly. Make sure you know what God says about what matters in a partner and what makes a marriage healthy. Second, how's your perception? Do you accurately see your own situation and the person you're interested in? Have you sought counsel from others? Have you taken the time to learn more about the other person's character? Don't follow your feelings until you've tested them.

The right time and age to start pursuing marriage will be different for each of us. But the one thing we should all have in common is waiting until romance can be guided by wisdom. Then we can experience the season of courtship at the *right time* and the *right pace* with a *clear purpose* and a *clear head*. This is romance at its best.

The Rest of the Story

Let me end this chapter with the conclusion of Rich and Christy's story. A month after Rich buried their love letters, both he and Christy left home for colleges in different parts of the country. They didn't say goodbye. They didn't write or call each other. Because their schools had different schedules, they didn't see each other during the year. Those were difficult days. The love they felt for each other hadn't gone away.

A year and a half after they'd broken up, Christy called her mom from school and told her that she was still struggling with her feelings for Rich. When her dad found out, he asked if she knew how Rich was doing. "How would I know?" Christy answered, the emotion in her voice thinly veiled. "I haven't talked to him since we broke up."

Her dad was impressed. Rich had stuck to his word and broken off communication with Christy. Mike decided to intervene once more. A few months later, when Rich was home from college, Mike called him and asked him to come to his office.

"I had no idea what he wanted to talk to me about," Rich says. "I thought I must be in trouble, but I couldn't imagine what I'd done."

As it turned out, Rich wasn't in trouble. Mike wanted to meet with him to thank him for keeping his word. He also wanted to tell him that he felt it was an appropriate time for Rich and Christy to begin a courtship.

Rich was floored. He told Mike that he needed time to pray about it. "Well, next week I have to go down to Richmond," Mike told him. "Why don't you drive me down, and we can talk about it then?"

A week later Rich and Mike were on the road again. It was just like old times. And it was time for another talk.

Rich had prayed hard that week about starting a relationship with Christy again. But as he sought God, he sensed Him saying that it still wasn't the right time for a courtship. "I still wasn't ready to get married. I was still figuring out what I'd be doing for a living. It seemed that God was saying, 'You committed to these principles, and you need to stick to them even if her dad is giving you the green light.'"

When Rich shared this with Christy's dad, Mike couldn't have been more surprised or more pleased. It was as though their roles had been reversed since their first talk about wisdom and romance. This time it was the young man who was sharing what God had taught him about waiting for the right time.

A Red Maple for Christy

Rich and Christy didn't begin a courtship then, but they did start to talk and ease back into a friendship. A year later, with Christy still away at school, they began a long-distance courtship. Things were so different this time. Their relationship was just as romantic, but now it had purpose and direction. They had their parents' blessing. Every day their confidence for marriage grew.

All that time the box full of love letters lay hidden. Rich had never told Christy that he had buried them in her own front yard. She thought the letters had been burned. The Christmas before she graduated from college she found out otherwise.

Christmas morning, Rich was celebrating at the Farris home. "This one's for you," he said, handing Christy a small box. She unwrapped it and found a nursery tag for a red maple.

"I bought you a tree," Rich told her.

"Oh," Christy said, trying to sound enthusiastic.

Her family, who by this time were all in on the surprise, could hardly contain themselves. "Why don't you plant it in the front yard?" her father suggested.

"Now?" Christy asked.

"Sure!" Rich said. "Come on." He grabbed her arm and pulled her outside, where the tree and a shovel were waiting.

"Where should we plant it?" Christy asked as they walked down the driveway toward the front of the yard.

"This spot will do," Rich said, pointing to the ground. He smiled at Christy, then raised his shovel and drove it into the earth.

One More Letter

I didn't tell you about one other thing Rich had put in that box before he buried it. When he carefully wrapped it years before, he placed one new letter on top of all the others. It was a letter Christy had never read. In it, Rich asked her to marry him.

So, Christmas morning, over four years after it had been buried, the box of cherished letters was unearthed and opened. And four years after it had been written, Christy read Rich's letter proposing marriage.

Today, Rich and Christy have a soaring story of romance because they were willing to be guided by wisdom. Anyone can have passionate feelings, but only those who seek God's purpose and timing can know the true joy of romantic love fulfilled.

Just ask Rich Shipe. In the very spot he buried his hopes, he saw them come to life. In the very place he knelt for a funeral of his dreams, he knelt four years later to ask Christy Farris to be his bride. And as he pulled an engagement ring from his pocket, he heard her answer, "Yes!"

Chapter Four

TELL ME HOW, TELL ME WHO, TELL ME WHEN!

How God Guides You to the Right Thing at the Right Time

When Claire Richardson found out that David Tate liked her and that he had asked her father for permission to pursue a relationship with her, she burst into tears.

They were *not* happy tears.

Claire was upset. Throwing herself down on the couch, she pounded the arm with both fists and yelled hysterically, "No! No! No! He's messing everything up! I've never thought of him like that. I'm not interested in him! Oh, he's messing it all up!"

Her reaction bewildered her parents. Since Claire and David were good friends, they assumed that she would at least *consider* the possibility of a courtship. But Claire already knew whom she wanted, and it wasn't David. She liked Neil—and Neil liked her. He too had spoken to her dad, but because Neil was several years away from being ready for marriage, Mr. Richardson had asked him to wait on a court-ship. So even though their relationship was on hold, Claire and Neil knew that they liked each other and were confident about their future together.

In Claire's mind, there was no possibility for a romance with David. He was her good friend—that was all. She'd imagined being married to different guys, but never to David. He was like a brother. Now she was sure that their friendship had been ruined. Why did he have to do this? Why did he have to like her?

She didn't even need to pray about it, she told her parents. "Of course it isn't right."

Our True Condition

What if the girl you like responded to your interest like Claire did to David's? What will you do if the wrong guy starts pur-suing you? Or the right guy doesn't?

The questions of when and with whom we pursue a rela-tionship—or in Claire's case, when and whom we allow to pursue *us*—can be confusing and uncomfortable. Most of us would prefer not to face them. Walking by faith isn't our idea of fun. We want the discomfort and risk removed. Before we make a move we want God to make the situation crystal clear.

Do you see the problem? Our mindset is: "God, tell me *who*, tell me *how*, tell me *when*—and then I'll trust you." What God wants us to see is that if He did this, our trust wouldn't be real. We want a definitive answer so we won't feel vulnerable, weak, and dependent on Him. But guess what? We *are* vulnerable, weak, and dependent on Him.

And it's only when we realize our true condition that God can demonstrate His strength and love on our behalf.

In this chapter we'll use one couple's story to illustrate principles that can help you with the *how* and *when* and *with whom* questions of courtship. But more important, I hope it reminds you that finding these answers for your life involves a journey of faith that you can't sidestep by reading a book. What you read here can help, but you still have to sweat through these questions in real life.

At this point I think you'll find the rest of David and Claire's story helpful. Your own experience will probably be different from theirs, but as you read about how God worked in their lives, I hope that you'll be encouraged as you see His faithfulness, His creativity, and *His* impeccable timing.

Ducks in a Row

David called Claire a few days after her parents talked with her about him. He didn't know about her negative response to his interest, but even on the phone he could tell Claire was less than enthusiastic. He decided to hope for the best and asked if they could get together to talk.

Though Claire politely agreed to meet and listen to what he had to say, she already knew her answer. "I just couldn't see how a relationship with him could be the best thing." She tried to pray about it, but her prayers were halfhearted. "Lord, if this is Your will, please change my heart…but *please* don't let it be Your will!"

She felt bad. She knew that David hadn't come carelessly to the decision to express his interest. David wasn't the careless type—he was thoughtful, methodical, and steady. Even his appearance revealed it: His black hair was always cut short and perfectly styled; his clothes were neat and ironed. He regretted the day his buddies discovered he kept his T-shirts arranged alphabetically. "Hey, David, can I borrow a T-shirt?" they teased. "A blue one filed under *K* would be great."

So you can imagine that a guy who alphabetized his T-shirts would be very thorough in deciding whether to pursue a girl. And David was. He wanted, as he said, "to make sure all my ducks were in a row."

He prayed about it. He evaluated himself and his situation in life. He talked to his parents and his pastor. He even wrote out a list of questions to help him determine whether it was the right time to think about marriage:

1. Am I prepared to lead my wife spiritually and serve her in every way?
2. Do I have proven character, and am I growing in godliness?
3. To whom and for what am I accountable?
4. How am I involved in the church? What are my gifts and ministry areas? What are hers?
5. Are my motives for pursuing marriage selfish and worldly, or are they to honor God?
6. Can I provide financially?
7. What do my pastors and parents have to say?

David prayed over his questions. He thought carefully about Claire. Besides being deeply attracted to her, he knew that she was godly and a woman of character. One by one the "ducks" lined up. David felt confident that God wanted him to take the next step.

David went to Mr. Richardson first. He knew that Claire would only consider a relationship with him if her parents approved of it. She looked to her dad to provide oversight and screen any guy who was interested in her.

David's conversation with her father had been encouraging, though somewhat mystifying. Mr. Richardson gave his permission for David to talk with Claire, but he told David that another young man had already expressed interest in her. "Since that relationship is on hold," he said, "I think it would be fine for you to let Claire know of your interest. I don't know what God's will is in all of this, but I'm confident that He'll make it clear to you both. Her mom and I will talk with her, and then you can give her a call."

Then Mr. Richardson said something that David would puzzle over for the next two years. "Go ahead and ask her...but don't take her first answer."

What was that supposed to mean?

Eight Weeks of Silence

Evidently Mr. Richardson had a hunch that his daughter would not immediately warm to the possibility of a relationship with David. And as her couch-pounding response indicated, he was right.

When David took Claire out to dinner, she listened quietly as he spoke about the qualities he saw in her that attracted him. He knew that she primarily thought of him as a friend and asked only that she prayerfully consider a courtship.

At this point they had their first major miscommunication. For whatever reason, Claire left the dinner assuming David understood that she wasn't interested, while David left thinking she was going to pray about it and get back to him.

What followed was two months of silence between them—eight long weeks in which Claire grew bitter toward David for having "ruined" their friendship and David grew bitter toward her for not "coming clean" and giving him a final answer.

"It was yucky," Claire remembers. "I was mad at him for disturbing my plans, and then, because I didn't want him to think I was changing my mind or even considering a relationship, I was rude and ignored him."

They participated in many of the same church activities, even played in the college worship band together, but they wouldn't talk to each other. David assumed that her answer was no but was upset that she wasn't telling him so. A once thriving friendship was now dead.

It's impossible to know how long this would have continued if God had not intervened. One Sunday at church the sermon was about how bitterness can destroy fellowship among Christians. Claire was sitting in the pew behind David. She knew that God was speaking to her. After the meeting she pulled David aside and made a tearful apology. "I'm sorry for the way I've acted the last two months," she said. "I've been bitter. I have not treated you as a brother. I've not been a friend to you. I've been selfishly ignoring you and running away from this situation. Would you please forgive me?"

David's own eyes filled with tears.

"When I saw that," Claire says, "I realized just how much my sin had hurt him."

David was relieved, but he also was convicted. "As she apologized," he says, "I saw that I had sinned against her in the same way. Yes, I felt that she had left me hanging. But God showed me that I too had been bitter. Instead of going back to her and asking whether she was going to respond, in my pride I refused to talk to her. I was no longer treating her as my sister and my friend. I asked her to forgive me too."

David and Claire were reconciled that day. The experience, though difficult, strengthened their friendship.

Wanting It Too Much

Though his friendship with Claire was back to normal, the experience of being turned down was still confusing and frustrating for David. Why had God made it so clear that he was supposed to approach her if He knew that she was going to say no? Hadn't all his ducks been in a row? He had a good job, he felt mature enough emotionally and spiritually, and the people around him thought he was ready. He *was* ready! So what was the problem?

David talked to his pastor, Kenneth, who listened patiently as he vented his frustration. "Dave, I think you've made an idol out of marriage," Kenneth told him.

"No, no, I'm past that!" David protested. "I prayed about it. I evaluated my heart. I was content being single before I approached her."

"That's good," Kenneth said. "But look at your response to her lack of interest: You grew bitter; you got angry. That leads me to think that you want marriage too much. It's become a little substitute god in your life, and when you didn't get it, you reacted sinfully."

John Calvin wrote, "The evil in our desire typically does not lie in *what* we want, but in that we want it *too much*." David realized his mistake. Marriage was a good thing. It was good for him to desire it. But God was mercifully using the difficult experience of having this desire *denied* to show him that he wanted it too much. He had been placing his hope for happiness in starting a courtship and getting married instead of in trusting God for his ultimate satisfaction.

Letting Go

Two years went by. During that time David prayed about other girls. At one point he approached another girl in his church about beginning a relationship. She also said no. "That was strike two," he says with a laugh.

One girl David wasn't planning to go to bat for again was Claire. Their friendship was stronger than ever, and he didn't want to endanger it. Besides, he assumed that she still liked Neil.

But David didn't know that God was bringing Claire's relationship with Neil to an end. "It was distracting both of us," Claire explains. She and Neil finally talked and decided that being on hold indefinitely wasn't good for either of them. "We decided that we needed to assume that nothing was going to happen between us."

Letting go of the relationship with Neil wasn't easy for Claire. The emotional attachments were strong. "I have all these feelings for Neil," she told Pastor Kenneth. "Can I change my feelings and emotions?"

"You can," Kenneth assured her, "but first you need to change the way you think about Neil. Then your emotions and feelings will follow."

"That was exactly what I needed," Claire says. "For two years I'd been thinking of Neil as my potential husband rather than a brother in the Lord. I had to renew my thinking and release my 'claim' on him. When feelings for him would resurface, I could usually pinpoint the cause as wrong thinking."

Things didn't change overnight, but slowly Claire's feelings for Neil subsided. "God used that time to teach me to trust Him with my heart—to believe that if the relationship with Neil wasn't His plan, He would help take it away and change my heart. And He did. He took the feelings away."

A few months after her feelings for Neil were gone, a most surprising thing happened. Claire began to be attracted to David. She began to notice his servant's heart, his humility, and his leadership. This attraction felt different from her prior experiences of liking guys. "Before it had always been, 'Here's the guy I want!' But this time I thought, 'Here's a man I could follow.'"

Despite her growing feelings, Claire didn't want to get her hopes up. After what had happened the first time, she doubted that David would take another chance on her.

A Different Kind of Peace

David remained unaware of all these changes in Claire. But one thing he knew—he still had feelings for her. In fact, he still often wondered what Mr. Richardson had meant when he said, "Don't take her first answer." Should he give it a second try? Would he risk losing her friendship?

As he contemplated these things, David was surprised to realize that he wasn't anxious. God had been changing him. Even though he wasn't always aware of it, even though he sometimes felt like his life was on hold, God had been steadily doing an important work in his heart. The guy who loved to have his "ducks in a row" had grown to trust God more than his own meticulous planning. The guy who longed for marriage was now bringing his requests to God with joy and thankfulness instead of desperation or complaining.

A key encouragement to him was Philippians 4:6–7:

Do not be anxious about anything, but in everything, by prayer and petition, with thanksgiving, present your requests to God. And the peace of God, which transcends all understanding, will guard your hearts and your minds in Christ Jesus.

Now his prayers about courtship and marriage were very different. *God, I don't want to be anxious about this area of my life,* he would pray. *I present my requests to You. I'd like to get married, and You know whom I'm interested in. But I'm trusting Your Word, which says that Your peace, which transcends understanding, will guard my heart. I want Your peace, not the peace I attempt to create.*

One day on his hour-long commute to Baltimore, David prayed, *God, what's Your timing for me to pursue a relationship?*

As he prayed, David suddenly realized that it was the first time he wasn't assuming that he knew who the girl was going to be. He had finally let go. "For me, it was evidence that God was transforming me," he says. "I prayed, *Lord, I need You to help me determine who just as much as when and how.*"

The Right Time in the Windy City

For David and Claire, the right thing at the right time came together on a trip to Chicago. They went with twenty-five other young adults to serve a newly planted church and do outreach in the city.

The night before he left, David and his parents got into a conversation that turned unexpectedly to marriage. His dad and mom asked him when he felt he would pursue a girl. They lovingly challenged him not to hold back because of fear. "Son," his dad said, "I think you need to get going!"

"Get going!" With those words ringing in his ears, the next day David and the rest of the group flew to Chicago. Was God speaking through his parents and telling him that it was time to move?

One evening in Chicago he started talking to Amy and Nicole, two girls he'd been friends with since high school. To his surprise the conversation turned to the topic of marriage. "So when are you thinking about pursuing someone?" they asked, giggling at their own nosiness. Amy and Nicole had no idea the weight their next statement carried. "David, you know we care about you. Well, we really just feel that you should get going!"

David could hardly believe that his two friends were

echoing the exact words of his parents. He began to tell them that he *was* content. He was really at peace and not in a hurry. As he talked, David realized the significance of what he was saying. He actually *meant* what he was saying! He really *was* content. He really *was* at peace.

And suddenly, in the midst of this God-given peace, David sensed that God was telling him the time had come to try again.

One More Try

David picked the last night of the trip to act. The group was walking through downtown Chicago. David wanted to time his conversation with Claire to happen as they walked across a bridge over the Chicago River. He kept to the back of the group and to his delight found that Claire was walking there too.

When they reached the bridge, he asked, "Claire, can I talk with you for a minute?"

"Sure," she answered. He seemed so serious.

They slowed their pace and let the others get ahead of them so they could have some privacy.

"Gosh, I can't believe I'm doing this...again!" David said and laughed.

Claire held her breath. Was he about to...? No...no, it couldn't be.

David began slowly and deliberately, using every qualification he could think of. "I was wondering if you would consider...praying about...the possibility of...maybe thinking about...possibly pursuing a relationship with me?"

Then, before Claire had the chance to respond, he rushed to assure her that she was under no obligation to be interested and that if she wasn't interested it was completely fine and that he would always be her friend if she said no—in fact, she didn't have to answer him right away…she could wait as long as she wanted…and….

"Can I give you my answer now?" Claire interrupted.

"Of course."

"My answer is yes," she said.

Standing there on the bridge over the Chicago River with his heart pounding in his chest, all David could find to say was, "Cool!"

On his third try he'd hit a home run.

Learning as We Go

I see many things we can learn from David and Claire's story. Let me share a few that seem the most important:

1. Remember, God is interested in the journey, not just the destination.

David wanted to finalize his readiness for marriage; God wanted to reveal idols in his heart. Claire wanted God to bless her choice for a husband; God wanted her to submit her emotions to Him.

It's a mistake to view the process of deciding how, when, and with whom we begin a relationship as something to "get through" so we can move on to courtship and marriage. God is in no rush. His interest in all this is not limited to getting us married—He wants to use this process, and all the questions and uncertainties it involves, to refine us, sanctify us, and increase our faith.

2. Don't overspiritualize decision making.

God used very practical means to lead David: a thorough evaluation of his own preparedness for marriage, the consent of Claire's father, the encouragement of his parents and friends, and his own sense of peace about asking her one more time.

C. S. Lewis once wrote a friend: "I don't doubt that the Holy Spirit guides your decisions from within when you make them with the intention of pleasing God. The error would be to think that He speaks only within, whereas in reality He speaks also through Scripture, the Church, Christian friends, books, etc." Though God speaks to Christians primarily through His Word, He confirms and leads us in many different ways. But we should resist overspiritualizing the steps He expects us to take to make choices.

God knows all things. He knows whom we'll marry before we meet him or her. But that doesn't mean our task is to discover what He already knows or to worry that we might miss His perfect plan. Our responsibility is to love Him, study His Word, deepen our relationship with Him, and learn to evaluate our choices in light of biblical wisdom. If we're doing these things, we can make our decisions in the confidence that we aren't somehow missing God's will.

Will we fail sometimes and make mistakes? Of course we will. But the possibility of failure should never paralyze us. Though it wasn't easy for David, God used Claire's initial rejection of him for their good. God works through our choices and actions—even our missteps—to accomplish His best in our lives.

On the other hand, I'd like to offer one caution to men: I'm not saying that initiative is not required or that sitting around waiting for the Lord to drop a wife into your lap is somehow godly. As the old saying goes, "Lack o' pep is often mistaken for patience." Neither should you mistake a lack of courage for wisdom.

3. Our romanticized ideal of what we want in a spouse is often different from what God says matters.

My favorite part of David and Claire's story is when Claire began to fall in love with David's character—not his image or his personality, but his *character*. At first David didn't fit her romanticized notion of what mattered in a husband, but then she realized that he was a man she could follow.

Claire's experience is a good reminder to us that we should very carefully examine our criteria for a spouse to see if they are in line with God's. The first nonnegotiable is that the potential spouse be a Christian. But that's not all that matters. The book of Proverbs ends with an entire chapter dedicated to describing the "wife of noble character." It says that a woman who fears the Lord is to be praised and is worth far more than rubies (Proverbs 31:10). God says that virtue and character matter most.

Why is this so important? Because those who choose a spouse based on external and fleeting concerns experience much grief. The book of Proverbs is dotted with reminders of how *bad* marriage can be. It tells us, "A wife of noble character is her husband's crown, but a disgraceful wife is like decay in his bones" (Proverbs 12:4). It warns us about the "sluggard" and the "angry man" (Proverbs 20:4; 29:22). It says it's better to live on the corner of the roof or in the desert than it is to share a house with a quarrelsome wife (Proverbs 21:9, 19).

We need to make sure that we don't let our own romanticized and foolish notions lead us into marrying a person who lacks godly character.

A Second Yes

Courtship is a season for two people to grow in friendship, to get to know each other's character, and to see how they interact as a couple. As we'll see in the next chapter, courtship isn't a form of preengagement. It's a time to consider the *possibility* of marriage and to seek to make a wise choice.

Some courtships end with two people deciding that they should remain friends. David and Claire's courtship ended with two friends deciding that they should pursue marriage. Claire answered yes a second time when, on Christmas Eve, David asked her to be his wife.

I got to attend their wedding. It was a beautiful celebration capped with a great surprise: David had arranged for a helicopter to land behind the church and whisk the newlyweds off to their hotel in downtown Washington, D.C. Talk about a dramatic exit!

As I stood with the other wedding guests and watched the helicopter lift off into the clear night sky, I couldn't help but marvel at the kindness of God. The boy who had felt the sting of rejection was finally holding his bride. The girl who had once pounded on her couch in annoyance at the thought of David Tate's liking her was now flying away with him on their honeymoon, more in love than she had ever imagined possible.

In their wedding program, Claire quoted a passage from one of her favorite books, *Anne of Avonlea,* by L. M. Montgomery. She had picked it because it so perfectly described their experience.

Perhaps, after all, romance did not come into one's life with pomp and blare, like a gay knight riding down. Perhaps it crept to one's side like an old friend through quiet ways. Perhaps it revealed itself in seeming prose, until some sudden shaft of illumination flung athwart its pages betrayed the rhythm and the music. Perhaps...perhaps...love unfolded naturally out of a beautiful friendship, as a golden-hearted rose slipping from its green sheath.

Perhaps after all our worries and questions, we'll discover that all along God had the right thing at the right time for us. Perhaps His plan is more wonderful than anything we could create by ourselves—whether it comes with "pomp and blare," or quietly, "like an old friend."

Perhaps...perhaps...we should entrust our questions of "how?" and "who?" and "when?" into His tender care.

part 2

———

THE SEASON
OF COURTSHIP

Chapter Five

MORE THAN FRIENDS, LESS THAN LOVERS

How to Grow and Guard in Friendship, Fellowship, and Romance

We were eating lunch at the Corner Bakery when my friend asked, "Did you hear about Wes and Jenna?"

"No," I answered as I poked at my salad. Wes and Jenna were two singles from our church who had recently become a "couple." "What's the news?"

"They decided to end their courtship," he said.

I halted a bite midway to my mouth. "Are you serious? Who broke it off?"

"I guess it was mutual," he said with a shrug. "They felt that God was leading them out of it."

"Bummer," I said.

He nodded.

Wes and Jenna were good friends. I thought that they'd make a perfect match and that engagement was imminent.

"It's just too bad when courtships fail," I said wistfully.

"Yeah," my friend agreed.

I was about to continue my melancholy remarks when it dawned on me how wrongheaded my thinking was. What was I saying? Wes and Jenna's courtship hadn't failed. Its purpose had been to find an answer to the question of whether they should get married, and evidently God had shown them that the answer was no. Just because that wasn't the answer I preferred didn't make the courtship a failure.

"Let me revise that last statement," I said.

"How's that?" my friend asked.

"I should have said, 'It's just too bad when courtships don't turn out the way I want them to.'"

Well aware of my bad habit of matchmaking, he smiled and winked knowingly.

"A toast," I said as I raised my glass of Coke in the air. "To our good friends Wes and Jenna at the conclusion of their *successful* courtship."

Right Definitions

What's *your* definition of a successful courtship? It's an important question to answer before you set out on the adventure of seeking God's will for marriage. Often we act as if the only successful courtships are those that culminate in a sparkling diamond ring and the words "Marry me!" But careful examination reveals how limited and foolish this idea is.

Think about it. Engagement isn't necessarily a good thing. Today many couples base their decision to become engaged solely on emotions or temporary passion instead of on reality and wisdom. Can a courtship that leads to an unwise union be considered a success? No! Or what about a couple who gets engaged after having had a courtship that was rife with selfishness, sexual sin, and manipulation? Successful? I don't think so. We can hope that their marriage will be better, but it's impossible to call this kind of courtship a success.

Growing and Guarding

It's clear that we need to refine our definition of success in courtship. Getting engaged should not be our overriding goal. What should be?

I believe that in a God-glorifying, wisdom-guided courtship we have two central priorities. The first is to *treat each other with holiness and sincerity*; the second is to *make an informed and wise decision about marriage.*

In courtship our goals should be to *grow* and *guard.* We want to grow closer so we can truly know each other's character, but we also want to guard each other's hearts because the outcome of our relationship is still unknown.

At the beginning of a courtship a man and woman don't know if they should get married. They need to get to know each other, observe each other's character, and find out how they relate as a couple. This is what it means to grow closer. But the fact that the future is unknown should also motivate them to treat each other with the kind of integrity that will allow them to look back on their courtship without regret, regardless of the outcome.

Second Corinthians 1:12 sums up what every Christian couple should be able to say at the end of a courtship:

> Now this is our boast: Our conscience testifies that we have conducted ourselves in the world, and especially in our relations with you, in the holiness and sincerity that are from God. We have done so not according to worldly wisdom but according to God's grace.

Instead of making engagement the finish line of courtship, our goal should be to treat each other in a godly manner, make the right choice about marriage, and have a clear conscience about our actions.

My friend Leonard, a single man in his thirties, was disappointed when Rita broke off their courtship. But because he had acted appropriately toward her, he had the peace that comes with clear conscience.

"Sure my pride was hurt," Leonard says. "I asked myself 'Why?' and 'What went wrong?' many times. But I consider our courtship a success because I was able to walk away from it praising God that I had served and honored my sister. I treated her with the respect a child of God deserves. To the best of my ability, my motives, thoughts, words, and actions were in the right place."

Balancing Act

Maintaining the priorities of growing and guarding make courtship something of a balancing act. You have the clear purpose to consider marriage, but you also need to fight the urge to assume that you're going to get married.

It reminds me of a high-wire circus act. Have you ever watched a performer traverse a wire a hundred feet in the air? If you have, you know that the secret to his safety is the balancing pole he carries. Holding it horizontally with both hands keeps the performer from losing balance and falling off the wire.

You could say that in courtship we're walking across the high wire stretched between friendship and marriage. The two priorities of growing and guarding are like the two ends of our balancing pole. We need to hold our pole in the middle for success. If we're too guarded, we won't move forward in the relationship; if we grow close too fast, we risk emotional injury or unwise choices later on.

There's a tension you want to maintain. Just remember that it's a good tension. If God leads you into marriage, you won't need to guard your hearts—you'll belong to each other completely. And believe me, you'll cherish the memories of your courtship walk across the high wire as an exciting, one-of-a-kind time in your relationship.

I'll never forget Valentine's Day during my courtship with Shannon. How wonderfully awkward it was! On the holiday for lovers, I wasn't sure how to address her. She was my friend, but then we were more than friends. So we were more than friends, but not quite lovers. I felt like I was back in seventh grade agonizing over the meaning of the words on valentines!

In a card I spent hours writing I asked, "How do you guard a girl's heart while attempting to tell her how special she is? Can you give her a rose as you thank her for her friendship?"

My questions captured the healthy tension of courtship. Can you give her a rose as you thank her for her friendship? It sounds funny, but I think you can. It's part of the process of letting romance blossom slowly under the watchful eye of prudence and self-control. You're more than friends, so you can determine whether you should join your lives in marriage, but you're also less than lovers—your hearts and bodies don't yet belong to each other.

Enjoy it. Don't rush. Don't despise or hurry the in-between time of courtship, even though you often feel the tension. Instead, treasure the season. Balancing the needs to grow and to guard during courtship is a necessary and fulfilling part of making the journey toward marriage wisely and with holiness and sincerity.

To help you on your journey together, we've included in the back of this book what we call "Courtship Conversations: Eight Great Dates," starting on page 223. It's a practical, purposeful, and fun guide for couples who want to make sure they're talking and living through the really important questions that come up (or should be brought up) in a healthy courtship experience.

For courtship to be a resounding success and a delight, we need to grow and guard in three areas: *friendship, fellowship,* and *romance.* Let's look at each one and see what it means to strike a healthy balance in each.

Friendship

The first and most important thing you can do in your courtship is to deepen your friendship. You don't need to worry about igniting romantic feelings immediately or figuring out whether you're compatible for marriage. Those things will work themselves out as your friendship develops.

Growing in friendship involves learning through conversation who you are as individuals. It's having fun together and spending quality and quantity time together.

When you're just starting out, don't stress yourself out trying to orchestrate incredibly entertaining or romantic dates. Relax and enjoy each other's company. Look for activities and settings that allow you to spend time together and talk freely. And don't limit yourselves to going out on dates. Look for ways to share the different parts of your life—the fun, the mundane, and the in-between. Work together *and* play together; serve side by side.

The strategic question to keep in mind is: How can you let each other see the "real you"? Whatever it is you love, whatever it is that captures your imagination, invite the other person into it—and ask the other to take you into his or her world too.

"I think of myself as a student of Nicole," says Steve, who's been in a courtship with her for three months. "I want to better understand who she is so I can be a better friend. A lot of what I learn happens when we're just being together and talking. But I've also discovered that I have to be intentional with my questions. During the day if I think of something I want to ask her, I'll write it down so I can remember to ask her when we get together."

Guarding each other's hearts during this time means making sure the friendship has appropriate *pace, focus,* and *space.*

The *pace* should be unhurried. Don't try to become best

friends the first week. Just like any other friendship, this one takes time and consistent investment to develop. Don't rush or try to force your way into each other's lives.

The *focus* of your friendship in its early stages should be on getting to know each other, not on creating premature intimacy and emotional dependence. In the beginning of your courtship, look for activities where the focus is on something besides being a couple. In your conversations and questions, avoid talking about the relationship. Instead, seek to learn about each other. Don't grab for more intimacy than is warranted. The focus will change as mutual confidence about commitment deepens. You'll earn access to each other's hearts over time.

The amount of *space* your friendship occupies in your life will also grow over time. In the beginning, be careful that it doesn't crowd out relationships with friends and families. Don't be threatened by the other person's outside relationships. Make room for each other, but don't try to monopolize each other's time; remember that premature exclusivity in your courtship can cause both of you to depend on it more than is wise. Be faithful to your current friendships and responsibilities. As the relationship progresses, you'll make more and more space for each other, but this should happen slowly and be done cautiously.

Fellowship

As your relationship unfolds, you want to make sure it has a spiritual foundation. For your relationship to be strong, love for God must be the common passion of your hearts. Courtship is the time to grow in your ability to share this passion for God and learn to encourage each other in your faith.

Growing in biblical fellowship involves sharing with other Christians the most important aspect of our lives—the reality of Jesus Christ and His work in us. It involves praying together as well as talking about what God is teaching us and showing us.

Men, it's our responsibility to take the lead in biblical fellowship. Find out how you can be praying for each other. Take time to talk about what God is teaching you in your individual walks with him.

There are many other ways to grow in fellowship. You can read Christian books together, talk about sermons after a Sunday service, and discuss how you're going to apply what you learn. During our courtship, Shannon and I read the book of Acts together and sent e-mails back and forth about what we were learning.

Another important part of fellowship is spurring each other on in righteousness. Nate, a young man from Great Britain, did this in his courtship with Clare by inviting her to point out any areas of compromise she observed in his life. "I would consistently ask if she saw any attitudes or behaviors that were offensive or dishonoring to her, others, or God."

Guarding the fruit of true biblical fellowship means increasing your love and passion for God, not your emotional dependence on each other. Your goal is to point each other to Him. All the ideas shared for growing in fellowship have to be guarded from abuse. We should never use spiritual activities as a way to grab for more intimacy than is appropriate for our relationship.

One couple I know wound up in sexual sin as a result of their extended times of "prayer" in his car. Others use the facade of "talking about spiritual things" to share very private details about themselves prematurely. Although there's a place for confessing areas of sin to each other and asking for accountability, this should never be of a sexual nature. Our primary source of accountability should be with members of the same sex.

Another part of guarding our hearts in fellowship involves making sure we're not trying to take God's place in each other's lives. If you're beginning to look to each other as your main source of comfort, encouragement, and courage, something is wrong. Remind each other to find your soul's satisfaction in God alone.

Romance

Our discussion of romance has been left till the end intentionally. Growing in romance should take place only when friendship and fellowship are deepening.

The essence of pure romance is pursuit—a man showing through his words and appropriate actions his care, affection, and sincere love for a woman and the woman responding in kind.

While romance is not the first priority in courtship, it's still important. Romantic feelings and the pure nonphysical expression of those feelings are an essential part of this time in a relationship. If God is confirming the wisdom and rightness of the relationship, romantic feelings should be seen as a good thing and a gift from God. Our goal during courtship is not to stifle our feelings of affection and love, but to submit them to God and to grow in and guard them.

Men, it's our privilege to be the initiators of romantic expression in our courtships. Throughout the relationship, it's appropriate for us to communicate "genuine affection" (Romans 12:10, NLT). Send her an e-mail during the day to let her know you're thinking of her. Give her cards and write encouraging notes. Give her flowers to tell her how special she is. Romance doesn't have to be fancy or flashy. The most romantic things a man can do for a woman are the little things that let her know that she's on his mind and in his heart. And remember, these skills aren't just for courtship. If you get married, it will be your privilege to keep pursuing your wife for the rest of your life!

Our guideline for what we do and don't do during courtship is that we never want our romantic expression to promise more commitment than we would be ready to express in words. It should grow as our confidence about marriage increases. The goal is to tell the truth about the relationship. It doesn't serve a girl if a man's romantic expression is too far ahead or too far behind.

During the first month of his courtship with Nicole, my friend Steve was so determined to guard her heart that he forgot to show through his actions how much he really liked her—and believe me, he *really* liked her! Steve was actually very confident that he wanted to marry Nicole, but Nicole interpreted his reserve as a lack of serious interest. This caused her to be very guarded, which in turn made it difficult for them to grow closer. Fortunately, Nicole's father and mother were providing oversight for the relationship. They saw the problem and intervened. One weekend while Nicole was out of town visiting her sister, her dad took Steve aside and told him that he needed to express his feelings more. "It would serve Nicole if you were a little more romantic," he said.

Steve was only too happy to oblige. He felt like a kid who had just been told he needed to eat more candy! The next day when he picked Nicole up at the airport, he was waiting at the gate with a huge grin and a bouquet of flowers. Steve has since been increasing his romantic expression through his words and actions.

Ladies, it's appropriate for you to respond to the guy's increased romance. Your goal should be to match but not outpace him. Nicole has done this in her relationship with Steve. As he picked up the pace romantically, she reciprocated. When Steve took a trip with some friends, she arranged little surprises and notes for each day of his travel. First she baked his favorite brownies and had a flight attendant deliver them to him on the plane. Then when he arrived at the home where he was to stay, his favorite ice cream was waiting in the freezer. (Do you see a theme emerging? Women like flowers; men like food!) Steve and Nicole are growing in romance at an appropriate time in their relationship and for the right reasons.

Gentlemen, when we know that we want to marry a girl, we can begin to actively seek to win her heart. God-honoring wooing is neither licentious nor manipulative. It's pure, it's sincere, and it's backed up by a desire for lifelong commitment.

What does it mean to guard our hearts in regard to romance? In my relationship with Shannon, the principle that guided me was simple. Romance during our courtship needed to flow out of deepening commitment. I refused to stoke the fires of romantic zeal before I knew I wanted to marry her. Doing so might have led to short-term enjoyment, but it would have deeply hurt her eventually. Romantic passion awakened without commitment can lead to sin and regret (see Song of Solomon 2:7).

A practical application of this principle is the question of when to say "I love you." If you feel love for the other person, should you verbalize it? Again, we must be guided by what's best for the other person. In some cases, saying "I love you" prematurely can be a very unloving thing to do. Unless those words are sincere and an expression of true commitment, they are meaningless and can cause great pain.

There's no hard-and-fast rule here. We need wisdom. I chose to save the words *I love you* for the moment I asked Shannon to marry me. I wanted her to know the words meant something—they were tied to my commitment to her. I wanted to spend the rest of my life loving only her.

I share this not to say that it's always wrong to say "I love you" before engagement. Other men I respect have said it earlier. In their particular relationships, it served the one they loved to let her know the depth of their feelings, and engagement followed soon after. My encouragement is to use caution.

The Excitement Continues

Couples growing in friendship, fellowship, and romance still have to think about their different roles as men and women, communicate authentically, and have a game plan for sexual purity. We'll talk about these issues and more in the following chapters.

Is it idealistic to try to be more than friends but less than lovers—to be cautious and careful in courtship? Yes, but that doesn't mean it's unrealistic. Someone once said, "Ideals are like stars. We will not succeed in touching them with our hands, but by following them, like the seafaring man on the ocean, we will reach our destiny."

I believe that, guided by the ideals to love each other sincerely and to consider marriage wisely, we can reach the destination of being lifelong friends *and* lovers in marriage.

WHAT TO DO WITH YOUR LIPS

Practical Principles for Great Communication

Only a few days after I bought my cell phone, the calls started pouring in. Unfortunately, they weren't for me. It turned out that my phone number had previously belonged to a Domino's Pizza shop. Now at all hours of the day and night people were ringing me with their orders.

"I'm sorry," I'd say, "but this isn't Domino's Pizza. Yes, you dialed the right number. It's just that now it's the number of my cell phone. No, I'm afraid I don't have Domino's new number. Yes, I'm sure they'll honor your two-for-one coupon. Bye."

Most people understood. What I found hilarious were the callers who refused to take no for an answer.

"I'd like to order a large cheese pizza," a lady told me.

"I'm sorry, ma'am, this isn't Domino's," I said. "You've reached my personal cell phone."

"How much will it cost?" she asked.

"I have no idea, this is not...."

"Well, when can you deliver it?" she persisted.

"I *can't* bring you a pizza."

"You don't deliver?!"

"I don't *make* pizza!"

More than Just Talking

Communication. It's not such a simple thing, is it? Besides the complications created by our sinful tendencies and the differences between men and women, we have to deal with wrong phone numbers!

Even the best relationships have their "cheese pizza" moments. These are the times when instead of talking *to* each other, we talk *past* each other; times when we're so easily offended that we spend our time arguing over the offense instead of the real issue; moments when we're so focused on ourselves that we forget that hearing isn't the same as listening.

A lot of people assume that since they know how to talk, they must know how to communicate. If only it were that easy. My experience with the calls for Domino's Pizza proves that clear communication involves more than just talking. I was talking to the lady who wanted a cheese pizza, but we definitely weren't communicating.

Why weren't we? Because communication is more than just speaking; it's listening. And it's more than just listening; it's understanding and properly responding to what we've heard. Clear communication occurs when two people know not only what to say, but when and how to say it.

Many couples assume that since they talk a lot and have romantic feelings for each other, they're communicating well.

That isn't necessarily true. It's possible to exchange thousands of words with people and never learn what they believe or value or feel. It's possible to fall in love with what you *imagine* someone is like, yet never see him or her for who they really are.

If you're in a relationship and considering the possibility of marriage, I hope that you'll read this chapter very carefully. Maybe the title made you think that it's going to discuss the proper timing and technique for locking lips with your sweetheart. Sorry—you won't find that here. The most important thing your lips can do right now isn't *kissing;* it's *communicating.*

We All Have Room for Improvement

Authentic communication is a skill that takes time, effort, and determination to learn. It also takes humility. The first step in getting good at communication is admitting that we're *not* good at it. We all need to humbly face the fact that most of us are novices.

Men especially often have a lot to learn in this area. But let's not dismiss our weakness as a "guy" thing. Instead, let's push ourselves to grow so we can bless the women in our lives and experience the joy of rich relationships.

And women shouldn't assume that they can't learn something too. My mom realized early in her marriage that even though she communicated well with my dad when they talked about ideas, principles, or concepts, she struggled when they tried to talk about her emotions.

Mom had been raised in what she describes as a "quiet

Japanese family," in which her parents and siblings rarely, if ever, expressed their feelings. Her primary outlet for communication had been at school, where she would debate issues in the classroom with her teachers and classmates. The result was that her communication skills were lopsided. Like a weight lifter who had only exercised one group of muscles, her ability to communicate was strong in one area but undeveloped in another.

My mom knew that if she wanted her relationship with my dad to be healthy, she had to be honest about her weakness. Improvement took time. "There were nights when we'd stay up for hours working through an issue," she told me. "If we'd had a conflict or disagreement, your dad would patiently draw me out about what I was feeling. At first I couldn't even articulate it. But over time I learned to recognize and be able to talk about what was happening in my heart."

Let me encourage you to ask God to reveal the places where your communication can improve. And if you start to see some areas of weakness, don't try to explain them away; just ask God to give you the grace to change it. God opposes the proud but promises to give "grace to the humble" (James 4:6). As you humble yourself, God's mighty grace will begin to transform you.

Five Principles for Authentic Communication

Do you remember the two central priorities of a God-glorifying courtship that we talked about in chapter 5? They were *to treat each other with holiness and sincerity* and *to make an informed and wise decision about marriage.* As we discuss communication during courtship, these two priorities should be our guiding lights. We want to be able to say with a clear conscience that our words were sincere. We want to see each other's character clearly and better understand each other's attitudes, values, opinions, and convictions about life.

Courtship is the time both to look for weak spots in your communication and to work to strengthen them. Our standard shouldn't be *perfection,* but consistent *growth.* The following five principles can help you improve communication in your courtship.

Principle #1: Communication problems are usually heart problems.

In his wildly popular book *Men Are from Mars, Women Are from Venus,* author John Gray uses a fanciful metaphor to explain why men and women have so much trouble communicating. He says that long ago Martians and Venusians fell in love and moved to earth, but when they arrived, they promptly forgot their diverse planetary origins. "And since that day," Gray writes, "men and women have been in conflict." But if I were to write a book on our communication problem, I would title it *Men Are from Earth, Women Are from Earth, and Our Problem Is Sin.*

Of course, men and women do bring different needs and communication styles to our conversations. But over and over again God tells us that the words we speak and the way we communicate is rooted in our inner person. Jesus said, "The good man brings good things out of the good stored up in his heart, and the evil man brings evil things out of the evil stored up in his heart. For out of the overflow of his heart his mouth speaks" (Luke 6:45). James asks, "What causes fights and quarrels among you? Don't they come from your desires that battle within you? You want something but don't get it. You kill and covet, but you cannot have what you want" (James 4:1–2).

Jason and Gina have been together for nearly a year, but their lack of real communication is beginning to strain the relationship. "She says I don't talk enough," Jason says. "But I can't change who I am. I'm not a talkative person."

Rob has told Leslie that her constant sarcasm bothers him, but she can't seem to stop. The biting remarks "come from out of nowhere." She's tried to tell Rob that since she grew up around sarcastic humor, it's just an unchangeable part of her personality.

Are people like Jason and Leslie beyond hope? No, they're not. But they'll never be able to change their ways until they understand that the source of their problems isn't ultimately their upbringing or personality; it's their own sinful hearts.

Our lips are merely the messengers of our heart. Our words flow out of what's inside us. We can't disassociate ourselves from the way we communicate (or, as in Jason's case, *don't* communicate). Though our upbringing and personality are factors, we can't blame them for what's wrong with us. If our words are selfish, sinful, or uncaring, it's because *we* are selfish, sinful, and uncaring.

The good news for sinful "earthlings" is that God has sent His Son to invade our sin-drenched planet and save us. And Christ has come not just to save us for heaven; but also to combat the rule of sin in our lives and relationships here on earth. We can experience real, lasting change in our communication if we're willing to seek God's help. We can't change by fancy methods. We can't change by mere willpower. But God's Spirit working in us can help us to "will and to act according to his good purpose" (Philippians 2:13). As we invite the Holy Spirit to change our hearts, our speech will be characterized by love, joy, peace, patience, kindness, goodness, faithfulness, gentleness, and self-control (see Galatians 5:22).

So though it isn't easy or comfortable for him, Jason is learning to view his lack of communication with Gina as a heart attitude that he needs to change. "My pastor has helped me to see that I was being selfish and lazy." As he goes after the root problem in his heart, Jason's behavior is starting to change.

The same has proved true for Leslie. Instead of focusing on her behavior and trying to stifle sarcastic comments before they leave her mouth, she's asking God to help her change the heart from which her comments flow. "God has helped me see that I am very proud," she says. "I consider myself better than other people. That's why I criticize and tear other people down. I might have learned sarcasm from others growing up, but I've definitely made the sin my own." Along with studying the Bible's teaching on humility, facing and repenting of her pride has helped Leslie change her way of communicating.

Principle #2: Your ears are your most important communication tools.

Why is it that when we think of communication, we usually picture ourselves talking? The answer is fairly clear. We think what *we* have to say is pretty important—more important than what others have to tell us. But often the best thing we can do with our lips is to keep them sealed.

Recently my dad told my five-year-old brother, Isaac, that God gave people two ears and one mouth because he wants us to listen twice as much as we talk. Isaac's eyes popped wide open. To him, the little proverb seemed the most astounding truth he'd ever heard. He loves to walk up to strangers and ask, "Do you know why you have two ears?"

It's a good question for those of us who want to improve our ability to communicate. We need to be reminded that our ears are our most important communication tools.

Are you quick to listen? Listening is an expression of humility and genuine concern for others. "I can't tell you," a girl said, "how many dinners I've spent with men who talk the whole time, then say over dessert, 'I feel like I know you so well.'" Authentic communication involves asking and listening. If we want to truly know and understand other people, we have to care what they feel and think, not arrogantly assume that we already know.

Do you listen carefully? Or are you simply waiting anxiously for the next time you can start talking? How often do you cut other people off or finish their sentences for them? If you want authentic communication in your courtship, be a listener. When you ask the other person a question, absorb the answer. Note not only the words used, but also how they are spoken. Ask follow-up questions. Care more about their opinions and ideas than your own.

The Bible tells us that a fool "delights in airing his own

opinions" (Proverbs 18:2). Don't be a fool. Listen twice as much as you talk.

Principle #3: Good communication doesn't happen by accident.

In Don and Susan's church a popular motto for young couples was "Twenty-Four Before." In other words, couples should date for at least twenty-four months before getting engaged. The idea was to discourage them from rushing into an ill-advised marriage. The problem with the little slogan is that if two people aren't working hard at clear communication, no length of time can ensure that they really know each other.

Don and Susan got married after two years of dating, only to discover how little they had actually communicated with each other beforehand. "Marriage was a huge wake-up call for us," Don says. "We didn't really know each other that well because our communication had been so superficial."

Susan agrees. "We developed a lot of bad habits before marriage," she says. "Our dating was mostly focused on fun activities. We hardly ever talked about what we felt or believed. Our physical relationship made us feel more intimate than we really were. When we did have a conflict, we'd always try to get it over with as soon as possible, even if it meant leaving things unresolved."

Taking your time in your courtship is wise. But don't assume that a long courtship means that you're communicating well. You have to be intentional about it. Communication doesn't just happen. It's something we have to plan for and work at.

We men should assume the responsibility of initiating

meaningful communication in our relationships. Don't just plan activities; plan conversations. Before you get together, think about some of the questions you'd like to ask her. What do you want to discover? Be curious!

When Shannon and I began our courtship, I was bursting with questions for her. I wanted to know everything I could about this girl. What did she love? What did she hate? What made her laugh? What made her sad? What kind of songs did she sing when no one was around? What did she order at an Italian restaurant? Did she like sushi?

In order not to overwhelm her, I had to pace myself and spread my questions out. I was always on the lookout for creative ways to spark a conversation. Once I bought a book called *The Book of Myself: A Do-It-Yourself Autobiography*. It had 201 questions designed to help people write their own life story. Using a black marker, I changed the title so that it read *The Book of Shannon…As Told to Joshua*. I brought the book along on a few of our dates and interviewed her. "What was one of your mom's traits that you admired?" I asked. Or "Who was the person that influenced you the most growing up?" Having Shannon answer these questions allowed me to understand more about her.

As you plan your dates, make sure you're giving yourselves extended periods of time to talk. Remember that you can be intentional and *casual*. You don't want the other person to feel interrogated or pressured by questions. Don't be demanding. Don't limit communication by switching to a "now it's time to talk" mode. Communication shouldn't be formal or forced—it should be a natural part of your relationship that weaves through all your time together.

Principle #4: The absence of conflict doesn't equal good communication.

"My boyfriend and I have the perfect relationship," I heard a girl tell her friend. "We've never had a fight."

I winced at the girl's misunderstanding of what it meant to have a good relationship. A widow I know realized that the absence of conflict in her forty-year marriage had not necessarily been a good sign. "I used to boast to friends about how well my husband and I got along," she said. "But now I see that part of the reason that we got along was because we never fought—and the reason we never fought was because we never really talked."

Our goal shouldn't be to avoid conflict, but to learn to work through it and resolve it in a way that honors God. In their book *Love That Lasts,* Gary and Betsy Ricucci share ten tips for communication that can help you when you're experiencing conflict in your relationship.

1. Learn to express your feelings and frustrations honestly, but without accusing or attacking the other person (Proverbs 11:9).
2. Choose words, expressions, and a tone of voice that are kind and gentle. Don't use speech that could easily offend or spark an argument (Proverbs 15:1).
3. Don't exaggerate, distort, or stretch the truth. Avoid extreme words like *never* and *always* (Ephesians 4:25).

4. Give actual and specific examples. If necessary, make notes before you communicate. Stay away from generalities.

5. Commit yourself to seeking solutions instead of airing your grievances. Getting even isn't the goal—you want to get things resolved (Romans 12:17–21).

6. Listen to what the other person is saying, feeling, and needing. Try to detect his or her underlying concerns (James 1:19).

7. Refuse to indulge bitterness, anger, withdrawal, or argument. Though these emotions are normal, indulging them is sin (Ephesians 4:26).

8. Don't hesitate to acknowledge your own failure, and be quick to forgive the other person. Make sure you don't hold a grudge (Luke 17:3–4).

9. Keep talking and asking questions until you are sure that you both understand clearly what the other is saying and feeling. Encourage each other as you press toward a solution (Romans 14:19).

10. Train your mouth and heart until you can say the right thing at the right time in the right way for the right reasons!

Remember, conflict is not necessarily a bad thing. And don't be surprised if you experience it. It's a sign that you're really getting to know each other. Don't run from it; instead, ask for God's help to humbly and lovingly resolve it.

Principle #5: Motive is more important than technique.

Finally, remember that it's very important to have a godly *motive* for our communication. Before we worry about method or technique, we need to make sure the motive of our heart is pleasing to God. He wants our motive to be to sincerely love and serve others—to build up, encourage, and benefit them. "Do not let any unwholesome talk come out of your mouths," Paul wrote, "but only what is helpful for building others up according to their needs, that it may benefit those who listen" (Ephesians 4:29).

Many books promise to help you learn to communicate so that you can get what you want. This approach turns words into weapons to further our own selfish desires, and the Bible tells us that this kind of communication is worthless. Paul writes, "If I speak in the tongues of men and of angels, but have not love, I am only a resounding gong or a clanging cymbal" (1 Corinthians 13:1). Heavenly eloquence is meaningless if it lacks the overriding motive of love for God and our fellow man.

A godly motive radically changes *how* and *what* we communicate in courtship. Instead of using words to gratify ourselves, we use them to glorify God and put the interests of others first.

You Still Need to Guard

In chapter 5 we saw how courtship is a season of being "more than friends, but less than lovers"—a time in which we need to grow our relationship and yet guard each other's hearts, since we don't know if we'll get married.

You will guard as you make sure that you don't promise or imply a deeper level of commitment or confidence in the relationship than you really have. In his courtship with Brittany, Kyle realized that until he was ready to propose, he needed to steer away from talking about "the future" as if they would be together then. "It wouldn't be fair to Brittany for me to say, 'Oh, wouldn't it be great if we had a house like that one day,' or even, 'Someday in the future we'll do such and such a thing.' It makes it hard for her to stay focused on where we are right now in the relationship."

Clear communication does not equal premature or inappropriate intimacy. During his courtship with Ginger, my friend Chuck consistently initiated what he called "heart checks." These were conversations in which he and Ginger talked about their expectations and concerns and their level of faith in the relationship. As the one doing the pursuing, Chuck knew he was responsible to be open about his feelings so that Ginger could have something to which to respond. This helped her to guard her heart and keep from being further along emotionally than Chuck was.

We have to be very careful that the words we say and the *way* we say them don't communicate more than we mean. Someone has said, "Don't write a check with your mouth that your body can't cash." In other words, "Don't promise more than you can back up with your actions."

Donna's relationship with Bill ended, but she's grateful for the way he cared for her by watching his words. "If he felt a conversation was heading toward a topic that wouldn't be helpful or was premature, he would reroute it," Donna says. "Once or twice he came back to me after we talked and apologized for something he had said that he didn't think was beneficial to me. I thought it was funny at the time, but now I realize it helped me guard against hoping prematurely that we'd get married."

As your relationship deepens and your confidence for marriage increases, you will want to begin discussing topics relevant to marriage. (We'll look at some of those questions in chapters 10 and 11.) But don't get ahead of yourselves. You still need to guard.

Be Courageous

The Bible says, "An honest answer is like a kiss on the lips" (Proverbs 24:26). I guess that gives us an idea of just how good authentic communication can be. It's a lot of work, but it's worth the effort.

As you read this chapter, perhaps you realized that you're afraid of honest and authentic communication. It's okay to admit that. It's a risk to let another person see who you really are. What if they don't like what they see? What if they end the relationship as a result?

Let me encourage you to place your confidence in what God is doing. He is at work in your relationship. You don't need to be ruled by the fear of someone else's opinion of you.

It is possible that honest communication will lead one or both of you to see that the relationship shouldn't lead to marriage. The thought of that might hurt, but think of the alternative. Do you want the person you're courting to fall in love with something you aren't? Is it really honoring to God or loving to the other person to fake who you are or hide your true opinions and feelings? Imagine the much better possibility that as you trust God and communicate well, the person you're courting will fall in love with the real you.

You can't love what you don't know. You can't be truly loved if you're not truly known. And the only way to know and be known by another person is to communicate—openly, honestly, sincerely, humbly. So let's be courageous. We know what to do with our ears and our hearts and our lips.

Chapter Seven

IF BOYS WOULD
BE MEN, WOULD
GIRLS BE LADIES?

How to Embrace Your
God-Given Role
As a Man or Woman

Recently I came across a book entitled *The Passive Man's Guide to Seduction.* I don't recommend it. The book's basic premise is that women today want to be the aggressors in relationships—they want to make the decisions and call the shots. In effect, they want to be "the men." Thus, the most effective way for a man to seduce a woman is to sit back, be passive, and let her take charge.

How romantic.

This couch-potato vision of masculinity is just one example of the current confusion about the role of gender in romance and courtship. And it's not just a secular problem. Christians are mixed-up too.

My friend Mike was shocked when a Christian woman he was close to proposed to him. "You know I'd marry you," she told him one day. "Do you want to get married? Look, I'll even buy the ring if it will make it easier."

Mike shook his head in disbelief as he recounted the story. "She was serious!" he said. "Women aren't supposed to do that…are they?"

The truth is that we're not sure how to behave. Men don't know what it means to be a man, so we lazily do whatever is easiest. Women don't know what it means to be a woman, so they end up acting like men. Relating to the opposite sex can be confusing when you don't know what you're the opposite of.

A Genuine Question

So far we've been talking about how a man and woman can honor God as they make their way toward marriage. But before we can go any further in our discussion of courtship, we need to grapple with the deeper question of what it means to *be* a man or a woman. What did God have in mind when He made two sexes? What is His plan? And how should His purposes for manhood and womanhood inform the way we relate in courtship?

The title of this chapter is a genuine question: If boys would be men, would girls be ladies? In other words, are we willing to step on God's scales and measure ourselves by His definition of mature masculinity and femininity? Few things could be more important in a courtship. Before we can glorify God in our relationships with each other, we have to understand and embrace the unique roles God has assigned us as men and women.

A Cast in Rebellion

For many people, the idea that a Creator assigns roles is offensive. They don't want any person, any religion, or any God telling them how to express their manhood or womanhood. They reject the idea of God-given roles and do whatever they can to blur gender distinctions.

The state of human sexuality today is like a play in which the cast is in rebellion against the playwright and his story. Imagine the chaos. The actors hate him. They reject their roles and mock the script. To show their contempt, some refuse even to read their lines. Other actors switch their roles and costumes to confuse the plot. Still others read their parts out of place, slur their lines, and lace them with obscenities.

This is a picture of the wicked and perverse generation in which Christians are called to shine like stars (Philippians 2:15). It's the generation of the "transgendered," in which men act like women and women act like men. And it's amidst this chaos that God wants His children to be faithful to the roles He has assigned us, even though the majority of humanity has abandoned them.

Just as a play is written by a playwright, the story of human history is written by God. The Bible teaches that our roles as male and female are part of the beautiful story God is telling.

Since God made us in His image, we reflect something of who He is (Genesis 1:27). Therefore, faithfulness to God's definition of manhood and womanhood is faithfulness to Him. Every scene we take part in—practicing biblical manhood and womanhood while single, in friendship with the opposite sex, in courtship, in marriage—is a chance to bring honor to the Playwright. In fact, the Bible tells us that the union of man and woman in marriage points to the climatic final scene—when Christ returns for His church, the bride He died to save (Ephesians 5:31–32).

This is why our roles as men and women matter. This is why we embrace our God-given differences and why we never want to lose them. God has made us male and female to tell a story too marvelous for us to fully comprehend. He has made the sexes different from each other to reflect a reality that existed before we did. Following God's script for our sexuality in every scene of our lives means that we are depicting the truth and faithfully telling *His* story. And when we do that, we experience the fullness of life that God wants for us as men and women. His plan leads to our joy and fulfillment.

The Roles Assigned in Eden

So what does God say it means to be man or woman? The Christian's first stop for the answer is the Genesis account of when God created the first man and woman. That is Act 1 of God's story.

Jesus showed us that the Genesis account should be the foundation of our perspective of true manhood and womanhood. When He was questioned about marriage, He pointed his questioners back to God's design: "Haven't you read…that at the beginning the Creator 'made them male and female'?" (Matthew 19:4). Paul did the same. When he wrote to the Ephesian church about how husbands and wives were to relate to each other, he referred his readers to God's original intention, which He revealed before sin entered the world (Ephesians 5:31).

From the first two chapters of the Bible we learn that Adam and Eve were created equal in God's sight. In our chauvinistic culture, in which women are often belittled and abused, this fact needs to be clearly stated. God made women totally equal to men in personhood, dignity, and worth. They are no less important or valuable to God.

Within the context of their equality, God assigned men and women different roles. He made Adam first, signifying his unique role as leader and initiator. He created Eve from Adam and brought her to Adam to be his helper in the tasks God had assigned him. She was made to complement, nourish, and help her husband. God's greatest gift to man was "a helper suitable for him" (Genesis 2:18). This doesn't minimize a woman's role, but it does define it.

Men and women were created equal, yet different. And the fact that we're different is wonderful. What a boring world it would be if the opposite sex weren't so mysterious, so puzzling, and at times so infuriatingly unlike us!

God didn't make us to duplicate each other, but to complement each other. The point here is not that Adam was better than Eve, just as God the Father is not "better" than God the Son. Father and Son are equal in essence, power, glory, and worth, but they have different roles; and the Son joyfully submits to the Father's will (1 Corinthians 15:28). So in marriage a husband and wife are equal, even though Scripture tells the wife to joyfully submit to her husband's leadership.

In his commentary on Genesis, Matthew Henry explained it beautifully: "Eve was not taken out of Adam's head to top him, neither out of his feet to be trampled by him, but out of his side to be equal with him, under his arm to be protected by him, and near his heart to be loved by him."

In Ephesians 5:21–33, Paul says that the husband's leadership isn't to be tyrannical or cruel, but kind and loving. Men are called to love their wives sacrificially and selflessly just like Jesus loves the church. Wives are instructed to follow their husbands just as the church obeys Christ. This is not mindless, joyless submission, but active participation and response to loving leadership.

Brother and Sister Before Husband and Wife

Guess what? You don't have to wait until marriage to participate in the beautiful harmony of God's plan for the sexes. Marriage doesn't make you a man or woman—you already are one. And God wants you to practice mature masculinity or femininity right now.

In 1 Timothy 5:2, Paul tells the single Timothy to treat younger women "as sisters, with absolute purity." Notice that he doesn't tell Timothy to treat younger women "like one of the guys." Timothy's masculinity is to be expressed in a unique way toward women: He is to view them as his sisters.

What this teaches us is that our gender roles are important *throughout* our lives. Before we're husbands and wives, we're brothers and sisters in Christ who rehearse together God's definition of masculinity and femininity. Gentlemen, we can practice tender, servant leadership *right now*. Ladies, you can practice responsive support to godly men in your life *today*. Side by side we can grow into the godly men and women God wants us to be.

Let's Be Men

First, I want to talk to the men. Men, we have our work cut out for us, and we need to take it very seriously. What business do we have pursuing a relationship with a woman when we still haven't figured out what it means to be a man? We owe it to the women in our lives, our future wives, and to God to figure this out.

Elisabeth Elliot, a woman I deeply respect, wrote to her nephew Pete, "The world cries for men who are strong—strong in conviction, strong to lead, to stand, to suffer. I pray that you will be that kind of man—glad that God made you a man, glad to shoulder the burden of manliness in a time when to do so will often bring contempt."

I want to be that kind of man. I have a long way to go. I fail more often than I succeed. I let my sin, my fear, and my laziness get the best of me. But I want to change. I know that God has made me a man for a reason. No matter what culture says, or even what some women say, I want to gladly "shoulder the burden of manliness."

It's not the easiest path. Earlier I told you about a book that encouraged men to be passive in relationships. According to the author, the only alternative to passivity is being aggressive and overbearing. Sadly, these are the two courses many men take. But God wants us to reject both of them. Biblical masculinity is neither passive nor rudely aggressive. God calls us to be servant initiators—firm but gentle, masculine yet caring, leaders yet servants. We're called to be protectors, not seducers.

Here are four practical ways you can do these things in your relationships with women.

1. Assume the responsibility of leading and initiating in your relationships with women.

Leading is a form of serving. When you provide direction, suggest ideas, and initiate conversation or activities, you're serving your sisters.

This doesn't mean that you treat women as if you were their husband and the one to lead them in important life decisions. Even during the season of courtship, this isn't your place. Until you're a woman's husband, she is under no obligation to submit to your leadership. If she has a Christian father, that protection and oversight should come from him. But while you shouldn't overstep your bounds, you can serve a woman (and win her trust for the future) by leading and initiating in small ways.

For example, you can serve your sisters by being the one to plan times together. This applies to a courtship as well as friendships with women. My single friends Jacob and Ryan frequently plan get-togethers at their apartment. They do the work of organizing activities and inviting other guys and girls to participate.

One woman told me what a burden it is when her male friends sit around waiting for the women to plan everything. "I don't like it when a man sits there asking 'So what do you want to do?'" she said. "I want them to make a decision!"

The same principle applies in your courtship. Do you initiate conversations? Do you carefully plan your dates? Are you thinking ahead and directing the course of the courtship? It's your job to make sure that it's continuing to grow at a healthy rate. It's your responsibility to make sure you're both guarding your hearts.

As you can see, servant leadership requires work. It means sacrifice. It means going out on a limb and proposing ideas, setting direction, and inviting others to follow. It means listening, taking others' interests and needs into account, and adjusting as necessary. It means deferring to others at times. Leadership isn't tyranny; it's service rendered. It's difficult, but it's a big part of what it means to be a man.

2. Be a spiritual leader in your relationships with women.

Men, we should set the spiritual pace in our relationships with women.

We should be the ones to make sure our relationships aren't merely superficial and entertainment oriented, but deep, God focused, and characterized by biblical fellowship.

The first important step is to make your own personal growth in godliness a priority. Don't be content to be spiritually lukewarm—strive to set an example of passion for God.

My friend Joseph sets a terrific example in this area. When he's with a group of friends, at some point in the conversation he'll ask a question like, "So what did you think of the sermon Sunday?" or "Can I share something God is showing me?" or "What's an area God is helping you to grow in?"

Do you know what Joseph is doing? He's initiating biblical fellowship. He's asking questions that help him and his friends share the new life they have because of Jesus. He's leading them in talking about the reality of God in their lives.

Joseph isn't a spiritual show-off. His goal is to serve his friends and enrich his own life. He knows how easy it is to let a whole night go by without having a serious, God-focused conversation. He knows that in fellowship he and his friends are truly growing closer.

Men, in marriage we'll be called to be the spiritual leaders of our homes. Before marriage, let's practice leading in biblical fellowship with friends and during courtship. Then we'll be that much more prepared to do so with our wives and children.

3. Do little things in your relationships with women that communicate your care, respect, and desire to protect.

This doesn't have to be complicated. Simply be a gentleman to the women in your life. Your goal is to show through your actions that their status as a woman is a noble one.

Let them feel your concern and respect in as many ways as you possibly can. You can do this through small actions: open the door for them, pull out their chair, escort them to their car at the end of a night. If you need more guidance, ask a few Christian women for pointers. You'll be amazed how willing they'll be to help educate you!

In your courtship, remember that you're not doing these things merely to impress or to win a woman's heart. You do these things for God's glory. You do them to serve a sister in Christ and honor her as a woman.

(A brief aside to women: If you're just friends with a man, and he's trying to treat you like a lady, don't assume he has a romantic interest in you. One of the fastest ways to derail a man's attempts to practice servant leadership is to interpret his actions as romantic overtures. As my friend Jen put it, "Girls should assume that until a guy expresses interest, they're just friends.")

4. Encourage women to embrace godly femininity.

Look for ways to encourage your sisters in godly femininity. When they make room for you to practice leadership, thank them. When they're humble and gentle, encourage them. Femininity is not weakness. It requires great strength of character for a woman to be gentle in an age that screams for her to do otherwise.

When you see a woman going against the grain of culture by cultivating a skill that will serve her family someday, compliment her. When a girl is pursuing a demanding career, but is still being feminine, let her know that you notice. Let her know you respect her.

We men should be the biggest encouragers and prayer warriors for women who are seeking to glorify God by practicing godly femininity.

A Challenge to the Girls:
Be Godly Ladies

Ladies, I hope you're still reading. I know that parts of this chapter might have made you cringe. "Women are supposed to respond to godly leadership from men? Give me a break!"

I think I can understand how you might feel. I'm sure that you can think of ways these biblical truths have been misused and misapplied by domineering and chauvinistic men. I'm sorry that has been the case. Please know that there are many men today who want to spend their lives proving that that's not what biblical masculinity is about.

Don't give up on us. We need your support. We need your prayers. We need you to fix your eyes on God—not on the men who have misrepresented His plan—and live your life in response to His commands for you as a woman.

Here are four ways you can be sisters to the men in your life and practice mature femininity.

1. In your relationships with godly men, encourage and make room for them to practice servant leadership.

If a man's biggest temptation is to be passive, a woman's biggest temptation is to take control. The man isn't setting a course, so the woman grabs the steering wheel. It might fix things in the short term, but in the long run it only discourages men from playing their God-given role as initiators.

You can encourage men to be men by refusing to do the work of leading for them. What you want to avoid is developing a *habit* of initiating in your relationships with men.

This doesn't mean that you never do so, but that it's not the normal pattern in your life. Neither does this mean that when you're single, you're supposed to submit to every man you meet. God asks a woman to submit only to her husband. But a single woman can, with men whose character warrants it, encourage servant leadership and respond to their initiative.

So if you're in a courtship, make room for him to lead. Step back and let him be the one to take charge. How else will he learn to lead? How else can you practice for the time when you will follow a husband?

Sylvia, who is in her thirties, gave me one example of how women can let men lead. "We ladies can be too quick to fill the silence in a conversation," she said. "We're like 'Oh no, he's not talking! I need to say something.' But I think it's important for us to let there be awkward moments of silence so the men can step up and lead the conversation."

Want some more examples? Don't plan your times together. Don't be too quick to be the one who "clarifies" the relationship—"What is our status?" If at all possible, make him do it.

And finally, be patient. Most of us men are pretty new at this. We usually aren't as skilled as you are at expressing our feelings. For a lot of us, courtship is the first time we've been expected to lead, communicate, and interact on an emotional level with a woman. Give us time. I'm grateful that in my courtship with Shannon, she gave me time to grow in my leadership skills. I made a lot of mistakes then (and still do!). I was often uncertain. But she didn't undermine my role or try to take over. Instead, she looked for ways to encourage me.

With God's help, you can do the same. When a man does lead, let him know you appreciate it. When he takes initiative in conversation, in activities, in fellowship—in any area—cheer him on.

2. Be a sister to the men in your life.

What are the categories you have for Christian men in your life—potential boyfriend, potential husband, no potential whatsoever? I encourage you to drop these categories. The first way you should view a Christian guy is as a brother.

Be a sister to the men in your life. Pray for them. Be yourself. Don't put up a front. Be a friend.

And remember, encouraging men to lead and to initiate doesn't mean that girls never start a conversation or have ideas for activities. My coworker Dawn and her three roommates make a practice of inviting a group of guys over for dinner every two weeks. They use these times to reach out to new people in their singles ministry and to develop friendships. Dawn and her roommates are being sisters to their brothers in the Lord.

3. Cultivate the attitude that motherhood is a noble and fulfilling calling.

Today many people scorn motherhood and the skills associated with managing a home. In our culture children are viewed as a nuisance, and motherhood is considered a waste of a woman's talents. A college counselor once told me that the majority of the female students she worked with secretly longed to get married and have kids, but they were too ashamed to admit it. What a tragedy!

Please don't believe our culture's lies about motherhood. If God has placed that desire in your heart, don't be embarrassed about it. The Bible encourages younger women to learn homemaking skills from older women. Learning to keep a home and love a husband and children is part of God's plan for the complete training of young women (see Titus 2:3). Don't hesitate to learn the practical skills that will one day allow you to serve a family. Search out godly mothers in your local church from whom you can learn.

You can possess biblical femininity without being married or having children. As a single woman, you can express your femininity by practicing hospitality and by caring for and nurturing the people in your life. But you can also honor God's plan for womanhood by agreeing that motherhood is a high and noble calling.

4. Cultivate godliness and inward beauty in your life.

A girl once wrote to tell me how God had used Proverbs 7:5 to convict her of being like the wayward woman who led men astray. "I don't want to be a seductress like her," she wrote. "I don't want flirtatiousness or immodest clothing to keep guys from seeing me as a sister in Christ."

If you want godly men to respect and cherish you as a woman, refuse to buy into our culture's obsession with being physically beautiful and sexually alluring. This is an attitude that springs from the motives of your heart and extends to the way you dress and act around men.

Is your wardrobe an expression of your love for God? Shannon often says to women, "There's a big difference between dressing attractively and dressing to attract." What's your motive? Have you ever asked your father or another Christian woman to honestly evaluate your clothing? Are you willing to sacrifice fashion to be obedient to God?

During our courtship, Shannon honored me by always acting and dressing modestly. A few times that meant getting rid of outfits that she didn't think would cause a problem (Ladies, you'll never know just how differently we're wired until you get married!). Once when I told her that a particular pair of shorts were a little too short and were causing me to struggle, she quickly replaced them.

In Scripture, Peter tells Christian women that their beauty should be that of their inner selves—"the unfading beauty of a gentle and quiet spirit, which is of great worth in God's sight" (1 Peter 3:4). In commenting on this verse, John Stott writes:

> The church should be a veritable beauty parlour, because it encourages its women members to adorn themselves with good deeds. Women need to remember that if nature has made them plain, grace can make them beautiful, and if nature has made them beautiful, good deeds can add to their beauty.

Grace will make you beautiful and will attract truly godly men to you. Make godliness and inward beauty your priority.

A Matter of Attitude

Earlier, I quoted Elisabeth Elliot for the men. Let me share another quote from her for the ladies. "A real woman," she writes, "understands that man was created to be the initiator, and she operates on that premise. This is primarily a matter of attitude. I am convinced that the woman who understands and accepts with gladness the difference between masculine and feminine will be, without pretense or self-consciousness, womanly."

My prayer is that you'll be this kind of woman—a woman who uses her gifts, develops her mind, and is passionate about God, and yet who is, without question, womanly. I realize that the attitude Elisabeth Elliot describes runs against the grain of our culture. In many ways women today are encouraged to be anything and everything they can dream of—except feminine and womanly.

But don't take your cues from our culture. Don't base your dreams or definition of success on a world that has rejected God. Instead, let God's Word define success. Your Father in heaven made you to be a woman for His glory. You'll find that His plan is more beautiful than anything this world has to offer.

For Him and His Story

If you're like me, you're aware that you desperately need God's help to be who He has called you to be as a man or woman. It's true. We can't do it in our own strength. We need His grace.

Being faithful to His plan will require faith, great courage, and the constant awareness that God, not you, is the central figure of the plot—the story of human history is all about Him.

God is the center of the universe. He created you for Himself. If you're a man, God made you a man for His glory. If you're a woman, God made you a woman for His glory. He gave each of you a sexual identity so that you could express your manhood or womanhood for Him, His way—and in so doing, point to His greatness and reflect His goodness.

This is what it means to glorify God as a man or woman. If boys would be men, would girls be ladies?

We can answer that question only if we strike out together on the adventure of obeying God's Word.

———

Chapter Eight

COURTSHIP IS A COMMUNITY PROJECT

How to Gain Guidance, Support, and Strength from Your Church and Family

I peered out my window into the cloudless sky and smiled. It wasn't going to rain.

Friends of Kerrin Russell and Megan Kauflin had been petitioning heaven's "weather department" for months that the sun would shine today. Their prayers had been answered. It was one o'clock, an hour before the ceremony was to begin, and the weather was perfect for an outdoor wedding.

All morning and afternoon scores of volunteers had worked feverishly to get everything "just so." It seemed that half of our church's congregation was helping in some way. If you had flown over in a plane, the church grounds would have looked like an anthill just after a child had stirred it with a stick. People scurried here, there, and everywhere. Ladies put the finishing touches on the decorations; a team of men tested the sound equipment; dozens of high school students under Mr. Drier's direction prepared food for the reception.

The result of all the hard work was breathtaking. The wide, open lawn behind the church had been transformed into a beautiful sanctuary—its ceiling was the hazy blue sky; its walls were maypoles from which sheer white banners hung and waved gently in the breeze. Rows of neatly arranged white chairs reflected the sunlight and glowed against the intense green grass. Every detail—from the flower arrangements to the gazebo where Kerrin and Megan would exchange their vows—had a dreamy, fairy-tale quality.

Sharing Joy

The decorations were beautiful and the weather was perfect; but when I look back on Kerrin and Megan's wedding, I think the most wonderful part was the amazing sense of Christian community that reverberated from it. Each moment of the day, from the preparations beforehand to the ceremony and reception, was a *shared* celebration.

The moment that captured it best was when Julie Kauflin, Megan's mother and her matron of honor, walked down the aisle. As she looked into the faces of her gathered friends, her eyes said, "Thank you for being here…thank you for standing by us over the years…thank you for celebrating with us." In turn, the message on the countenances of the guests was: "We rejoice with you…your joy is ours."

We were more than just witnesses; we were participants. We were the friends, teachers, grandparents, mentors, uncles, aunts, and pastors who had taught, counseled, cried with, laughed with, and prayed for Kerrin and Megan from their infancy through adulthood. They were part of us—we each carried a special piece of their story. We had come to mark this moment in their life, to share it with them, and in sharing it, to multiply its joy.

We were celebrating not only that Kerrin and Megan would belong to each other forevermore, but that *we,* the friends and family who gathered to witness their union, belonged to them and they to us. "So in Christ we who are many form one body," wrote Paul, "and each member belongs to all the others" (Romans 12:5). Because of Jesus, we were a spiritual family so interconnected that it was impossible to tell where the bride and groom's joy ended and ours began.

Empty Chapel

While most of us can appreciate the importance of community at a wedding, what I want to show in this chapter is that community is just as important during the season of courtship. If a wedding is a community event, courtship should be a community project.

What made Kerrin and Megan's wedding day so beautiful was that it was the culmination of a relationship that embraced the church community at every stage. Their friendship grew while they were serving with others in the youth ministry. When Kerrin began to like Megan, he sought counsel from his parents, pastor, and trusted friends; before he expressed his interest to her, he met with Megan's father, Bob, and asked for his permission to begin a courtship. Megan agreed to the courtship only after getting advice from her parents and close girlfriends from church. During their courtship and subsequent engagement, they both were accountable to their parents and pastors.

Kerrin and Megan didn't just invite other people to share their wedding day. Much earlier they had invited them to participate in their love story. The health and success of their courtship and subsequent marriage was integrally linked to the support, love, and strength they received from their church and family. "No man is an island," John Donne wrote. The same can be said of a man and woman in love. No *couple* is an island. A healthy relationship cannot be isolated from the people around it.

A courtship devoid of community is like a wedding without guests. Can you imagine that? Try to picture a ceremony where only the bride and groom are present. There are no bridesmaids or groomsmen, best man, maid of honor, flower girl, or even a pastor to officiate. The chapel is empty and silent. The groom in his tuxedo stands at the altar alone; the bride walks unaccompanied down the aisle. She wears a stunning white dress, but there's no one to admire it, no one to rise as she walks by, no one to give her away to her groom.

Why is there something deeply troubling about this idea? Because a wedding with no one there to share it is no wedding at all! A wedding is the sacred exchange of vows before witnesses. In the same way, a courtship is more than just one man and one woman joining their lives together. It involves the physical and spiritual family to which they're connected—the community of people who witness, affirm, protect, and celebrate their love.

What Community *Doesn't* Mean

At this point you might be scratching your head. Maybe the idea of community in relationships sounds strange. Maybe your experience of church life looks nothing like this. I understand how you feel. Many of us are accustomed to shutting others out of our lives. What I hope you'll consider is that when we do this, we shut out the joy, wisdom, and encouragement that God wants us to have.

The place of community in Christian romance is both biblical and beautiful. As you take a closer look, I think you'll discover that embracing community can actually increase your enjoyment of courtship and your opportunity for a long-lasting, deeply romantic, and God-glorifying relationship.

But before we go any further, I want to make sure that you're clear on what I'm *not* saying. First, I'm *not* saying that you should sacrifice all privacy in your relationship. Having time alone as a couple is very important. Second, I'm not saying that you should have someone else (your parents or pastor) make the decision about whom you marry. Only you can make that final choice.

Our problem today is that we've allowed the importance of privacy and personal choice to cause us to neglect what the Bible teaches us about our need for fellow Christians in the local church. While it's true that no one else should decide whom we marry, how arrogant it is to think that we can make this important decision on our own without counsel and advice from others! And while a couple needs time alone, how shortsighted and foolish it is to cut ourselves off from the wisdom and support of the people who know us best.

Throughout Scripture, God reminds us that we weren't meant to live the Christian life on our own in any part of life—we need others in order to be holy, strong, and faithful. God has adopted us into a new *family.* Together we're called to be a holy *people,* not merely holy individuals (Ephesians 5:3).

While people in the secular world grow increasingly isolated, God tells us that He's building us together as His church to become a dwelling in which He lives by His spirit (Ephesians 2:22). "You are no longer foreigners and aliens," says Paul, "but fellow citizens with God's people and members of God's household" (Ephesians 2:19). "And let us consider," the author of Hebrews writes, "how we may spur one another on toward love and good deeds. Let us not give up meeting together, as some are in the habit of doing, but let us encourage one another—and all the more as you see the Day approaching" (Hebrews 10:24–25).

What Community Provides

The Bible points us back to the priority of the local church and our need for encouragement and strength from other Christians in *every* part of life—including romance. Our approach to romance should reflect the *radically different* relationships we have as Christians in the community of the redeemed. We weren't called to make it alone—we really do need each other.

How do we need others during courtship? Here are three important things community provides.

1. Community reminds us of reality.

There's nothing like romance to cloud a person's view of reality. When our emotions and feelings are in gear, it's difficult to be objective—to see ourselves, the other person, and our situation accurately.

Community provides reality checks in several different ways.

For example, it provides another perspective of our relationship. If it hadn't been for the reality check of a friend's advice, Kerrin and Megan might never have started their courtship. You see, when Megan found out from her dad that Kerrin was interested in her, she almost turned him down. He just wasn't her type. But a conversation over lunch with her friend Claire (the same Claire you read about in chapter 4) helped her see what qualities really mattered in a husband, and it changed her perspective.

One of Megan's journal entries from that time shows the slow transformation that took place as her friend gently challenged her to reconsider her attitude toward Kerrin. Megan wrote:

> On Wednesday, I went out with Claire. At that point I was in total confusion about Kerrin. My mind and heart were playing games. I spilled it all out to her and expressed the pros and cons and confusion.
>
> She listened and laughed at me. She told me about her experience with David and how he too was different from other guys she'd liked. Then she explained how it was qualities like humility and servanthood that drew her heart. As I listened, I realized

that all my life I've based my relationships on feeling and attraction. Claire emphasized that this decision of courtship and marriage *can't* be based on feelings. We are fickle people. Julie had told me the same thing: "You can't trust your affections, but you can rely on love and character."

Their advice shook up my romantic ideals and started me thinking about character. Then Claire asked if other people's opinions factored into my decision. I realize just how much this played into my initial decision to say no to Kerrin. I guess I thought I deserved better. It's just foolish pride. The more Claire described her experience with David, the more I saw that my ideals were all wrong. I left determined to reevaluate what formed my opinions.

Claire didn't convince me that I should court Kerrin; she helped me evaluate what played into my decision and why I thought and felt the way I did. I talked to Mom and Dad that night, still very much unclear and lacking faith, but determined to search my heart.

Megan's journal shows how God used a friend's words to gently prod her in the right direction. Megan was confused. She felt overwhelmed by her emotions. Like someone stumbling through a fog-shrouded valley, she needed others standing on the hills above the valley to call out to her with guidance. Megan's girlfriend Claire and her parents didn't make the decision for her, but by providing a reality check from outside the fog of her feelings, they helped her find her way out.

Another way that community provides us with reality checks is by giving us real-life contexts in which to observe each other. One-on-one dates are great, but if they're the only setting in which two people interact, chances are that neither is getting an accurate picture of who the other person is.

This is why it's so helpful to get to know each other in the midst of community settings like family, friends, and church. You could call these our natural habitats. If you want to understand the true nature and character of a lion, don't go to the zoo—go to the plains of Africa! There you'll witness his real temperament, abilities, and behavior. In the same way, when we see each other in the real-life settings of community, we're much more likely to see who a person really is—the person he or she will revert to once the restraints of dating and courtship are past.

This is where spending time together with your families is so important. Some people mock this idea. They think it seems old-fashioned, even childish. But interacting with each other's parents gives a couple a much needed reality check. For example, don't assume that if the guy you're courting is disrespectful and rude to his mother, it's the exception and not the norm. The truth is that the way he's treating *you* right now is the exception—the way he acts around his family is who he really is. This principle also applies to how the other person behaves around friends. If you want a clear picture of each other, you need to make sure you're building your relationship amidst the reality of community—not just when you're alone on romantic escapades.

Inviting Reality Checks

How do you embrace the reality checks that community can provide your relationship? One way is to make sure that your times together are balanced, with time alone and time with friends and family. At the beginning of your relationship, it might be wise to give even more time to settings that involve other people.

Next, invite reality checks from as many different sources as possible. Don't wait for your friends, parents, or pastors to come to you with counsel about your courtship—you go to them. Who are the people in your life whose lives demonstrate wisdom? Whoever they are, seek them out and involve them. Ask for their perspective and prayer.

My friends Brian and Sarah, who live in Orlando, sought these kinds of reality checks from their parents and other godly couples in their church. Before they got engaged, they systematically scheduled dinners with five different married couples. With each one they asked, "What is your honest opinion of our relationship? Have you observed anything that concerns you? Would you advise us to continue toward marriage?" What were Brian and Sarah doing? They were seeking the perspective of husbands and wives they respected and who had observed their relationship up close.

Finally, don't ignore what the reality checks of community reveal. If an overwhelming number of trusted counselors have reservations about your relationship, you should take that very seriously. Don't assume that the problems or challenges they see will magically disappear because you get married.

2. Community provides protection.

In a recent *Reader's Digest,* a mother told an amusing story that illustrates how community can provide protection in relationships. One evening this woman and her husband went with friends to the restaurant where their teenage daughter, Misty, was working as a waitress. A man at a nearby table, who was probably fifteen years older than Misty, began flirting with her. She ignored his request for her phone number, but he persisted. Finally she stopped what she was doing and leveled her gaze at him. "Do you see that man?" she said, motioning toward her father. The patron turned in her parent's direction. "That's my dad," Misty continued. "We have the same phone number. If you want it, get it from him."

While the story is humorous, I think that the principle behind it is very serious. I believe that every girl should have a godly man in her life toward whom she can point prospective suitors (good or bad) and say, "If you're interested in *me,* talk to *him!*" We need community because we need protection.

While I am aware of cases where men need to be protected from dangerous women, I make this point primarily to emphasize the importance of protecting the woman in the relationship. Today the most heartbreaking consequence of the lack of community involvement in relationships is that women are increasingly vulnerable. Look around at the date rape and the emotional and physical abuse women suffer. Where are the fathers? Where are the brothers? Where are the godly men who take up those roles for the fatherless?

One of the great privileges of godly manhood is providing

protection for women. As we talked about in chapter 7, this isn't a demonstration of our superiority, but an expression of our God-given role as servant protectors and leaders. Earlier I shared how my friend Kerrin met with Megan's father, Bob, to ask permission to start a courtship. It's important that you understand that this was something Megan *wanted*. She trusted her father and had invited his oversight and leadership. She wanted him to screen the guys who were interested in her. She wanted him to provide oversight during courtship. When Bob gave Megan away on her wedding day, it was more than just tradition—it symbolized the reality that she was going from his protection to Kerrin's.

Ladies, despite what you may have experienced at the hands of your earthly father, know that this is the heart of your heavenly Father for you. You were never meant to be unprotected. I'm sorry that many of you have never had a Christian father like this to care for you. I'm sorry that negligence on the part of men has left you vulnerable to mistreatment and abuse. I'm sorry that you've had to assume the masculine traits necessary to fight for yourself and be your own protector.

That isn't God's plan—it's the consequence of our sin and disobedience. Jesus came to reverse the effects of sin. Part of the reason He's given us the local church is to give fathers to the fatherless. God has given us the local church to be the spiritual family that can fill in where our natural family is lacking. My friend Karen lost her father to cancer when she was twenty-six. When she started a courtship with Alex, she asked her brother-in-law, Tom, who was also a member of her church, to play the part of protector.

"If Tom weren't in the picture, it would be just Alex and me," Karen says. "The truth is that I don't completely trust myself. I really need Tom's counsel. I need a buffer between Alex and my emotions. I need someone to challenge my perspective as well as to stand up for me."

Inviting Protection

Let me encourage you to take the steps necessary to invite the protection that community can give your courtship.

If the girl you're interested in has a Christian father, he should be the first person you schedule a meeting with. Getting his permission to pursue a relationship with his daughter will honor him and help protect her. Gratefully acknowledge his authority and leadership in her life. Make your case for a courtship and trust that God will work through him for your good. Don't try to undermine his leadership—honor it even if it means waiting longer or doing things differently than you had planned.

If, as the woman in the relationship, you have a godly father (even if you're not living at home), I encourage you to involve him in this part of your life. Talk to him and your mom about the kind of husband you're praying for. Get their counsel. Draft your dad as your personal "boy screener." Let him know who's on your list of possibilities and whom he can politely decline.

You might be thinking, But this doesn't work in my situation! I understand, and I hope you see the *principle* involved. Different people will apply it differently in their lives.

For example, I didn't talk to Shannon's dad before I told

her of my interest in her. She wasn't living at home, and though she has a wonderful father, he wasn't a Christian or providing spiritual leadership in her life. I knew that calling him to get permission for a courtship would be more confusing than helpful.

So instead, I talked to Shannon's pastor, as well as two other married couples from our church who were close to her. I made sure that they didn't have concerns about me or the timing of a relationship. Only after getting their encouragement did I talk to Shannon.

Then I called both Shannon's parents the following day to let them know about our courtship and invite their participation. "I'd like you to be involved in our relationship," I told each of them. I also told both her dad and mom that I'd talk to them before I proposed.

Do you see the principle at work in our situation? I was inviting the protection of the godly men and women who cared for Shannon spiritually, and I was honoring the father and mother who had raised her. We don't all have the perfect family situation, but we can all apply this principle in some form.

3. Community provides accountability.

Christian accountability is inviting others to help us live by what we know is right. It's asking them to challenge, to inquire, and to question us so that our actions line up with our convictions.

The Bible is packed with reminders of the reality of indwelling sin. Jeremiah 17:9 says, "The heart is deceitful above all things and beyond cure. Who can understand it?"

In 1 John 1:8 we're told, "If we claim to be without sin, we deceive ourselves and the truth is not in us."

The fact that our own hearts will betray us points us to our great need for fellow Christians to help us fight the fight of faith and resist sin. That's the reason Steve and Jamie, who are both in their late thirties, asked for accountability from Walt and Brenda, the older married couple who lead their home group. Even though Steve and Jamie are both single parents who have been married before, they wanted to be serious about sexual purity.

"When you've been married and have three kids, it's easy to think that guarding yourself against sexual sin isn't that important," Jamie says. "You can think to yourself, *Hey, I'm a big girl and I know the ways of the world.* But if you really knew the ways of the world and the consequences of sin, you'd be running."

Steve agrees. "I need help to guard my thought life. I want to be pure in my courtship with Jamie. Knowing that Walt will ask 'How's your behavior?' every Sunday gives me extra motivation."

Accountability is important for more than just maintaining sexual purity. The balancing act of growing and guarding that we discussed in chapter 5 is another area where others can help. Your parents, friends, or pastor can ask you how you're doing at guarding your communication and expressions of romance.

I encourage you to be accountable together to a married couple (ideally your parents) as well as separately to individuals. The couple you're accountable to should be a husband and wife you respect and who are willing to challenge and confront both of you when necessary. The person you're accountable to individually should be a godly man or woman of your own gender with whom you can talk easily and frequently and who is strong in the areas where you're weak. After all, accountability isn't helpful when the one who's holding you accountable is sinning in all the same ways you are!

This Isn't Arranged Marriage

Just as no courtship should be disconnected from the involvement of others, neither should it be controlled or manipulated by other people. A biblical attitude is one that humbly seeks the help of others. But this doesn't mean that we should rely on others to make the final decision about whom and when we marry. The very serious and binding commitment of marriage is something that only we can live out and stand by in the years to come. And for this reason no one—not parents, pastors, or friends—can make it for us. While their counsel should inform us, we are the ones who must hear from God and have faith to get married.

While many singles lack Christian parents, others have them but are confused about how much say they should have in courtship and marriage. I've come across some very sad stories of parents who manipulated and tried to control their children in courtship. This is wrong and unbiblical.

What principle can guide us in these questions? The Bible makes it clear that a dependent child is called to obey his parents as long as they're not asking him to disobey God (Ephesians 6:1). When we reach adulthood, we are no longer commanded to obey them, but we are called to honor them (Exodus 20:12). This means that we need to respect their counsel and consider it carefully.

Obviously our respect for their counsel also depends on the holiness and integrity of their lives. God has blessed me with a father and mother who have served God and been faithfully married to each other for over twenty-five years. For me, their counsel carries a lot of weight. They never told me what to do in my courtship with Shannon, but they were my most trusted counselors. And because they were humble and cared for me, they also encouraged me to seek the counsel of others.

Proverbs 15:22 says, "Plans fail for lack of counsel, but with many advisers they succeed." The decision of whom you marry should involve *many* counselors. If your parents are godly and the fruit of their lives demonstrates wisdom, they should be at the top of your list of counselors. But this doesn't mean that their perspective should be the deciding one for you. You should also pursue the advice of other wise counselors and form your own conviction before God.

In my own life the care and oversight my pastors gave me was essential to the success of my courtship. Their prayer, accountability, and counsel before and during the courtship helped Shannon and me keep the right focus in the relationship. I encourage you to get similar help during your relationship. Good, biblical leaders will be honest and forthright, but not intrusive.

Sharing Joy

God's plan for community in courtship is not about smothering your happiness. It's about multiplying your joy! Doesn't a sunset that you're able to marvel at with a friend seem even more beautiful than the one you watch alone? When we share something with others, we increase our own enjoyment. This is one of the sweetest motivations for embracing the involvement of your family and your local church in courtship.

When you're growing in your love for someone, it's wonderful to watch your friends and family falling in love with that person too. You'll see this joyful experience unfolding for Megan in the following excerpt from her journal. She wrote this four months into her relationship with Kerrin (and a month before he proposed):

Christmas is here. Yesterday we cut down our tree; today did some more shopping—me, Kerrin, and Chelsea. What a uniquely exciting time it is this year. Kerrin adds a whole new dimension to our family. Last night was this "moment"—decorating the tree with carols playing in the background, the family, and Kerrin.

Out of all the unexpected surprises in this season, the best is the inclusion of Kerrin in our family. It brings me such pleasure to see him embraced in our family. To see him as a part of all our traditions...joking around with Jordan, teasing Chelsea, playing with Brittany and McKenzie. I love watching him enter into our world, our life.

I didn't expect this to happen. I guess in my selfishness, I never really thought about this aspect of our relationship. How grateful I am for the time he's invested in our family so that they can grow to love him like I do. I love our times alone, but when I think of our times with the family—playing cards, watching movies, Starbucks, games, talking, laughing—I wouldn't trade a thousand date nights for those special moments.

Why do we need community for a successful courtship? Because we really do need one another.

We need to be reminded of reality.

We need protection.

We need help to be and do what we believe.

Thank God we're not alone. Jesus has bought our freedom by His death and resurrection. He's reconciled us to Himself, and He's reconciled us to each other. We're family—brothers and sisters.

Why do we need community? Because like a good wedding, courtship is meant to be a shared celebration.

Chapter Nine

TRUE LOVE DOESN'T *JUST* WAIT

How to Be Passionately in Love and Sexually Pure

Who are you kidding?"

I shifted slightly, shut my eyes, and tried to ignore the voice. "You're not fooling anyone," it said again.

Still I didn't answer. Maybe he would go away. Give up.

Shannon and I had gotten engaged two months earlier. We'd come to visit her mother, Mitzi, at her Ocean City beach house. It was a well-deserved break from wedding planning and work. Didn't my conscience need a break too? He'd been working overtime these past few months. Couldn't he ease up a little? Relax?

"This is ridiculous, Josh," he said again, undeterred. "You know this is wrong." Evidently he didn't do vacations.

He was right. I knew he was right, but I was too stubborn to admit it. It had been my idea for Shannon and me to take an afternoon nap in the outdoor hammock. As soon as I suggested it, I knew it was a bad idea. My ulterior motive was to get as close to Shannon's body as possible. My conscience was incensed. "Take a nap in a hammock?!" he screamed. "Are you nuts? That's not fleeing temptation—that's inviting it!"

Chill out, I said to him as Shannon and I grabbed two pillows and headed to the hammock hanging between two trees. *Have you ever heard of Christian freedom?* I continued testily. *We're engaged, all right? This is innocent.* "To the pure all things are pure."

"Don't quote Scripture to me, bucko!" he yelled. "Would you do this if your pastor were here? Would you put this in a book? Would you write, 'As you strive for purity, snuggle up together for a nap in a hammock'?"

I am not a legalist, I shot back as Shannon and I steadied the swaying contraption, climbed in, and lay down with our heads at opposite ends. *I will not live my life by other people's standards,* I told my conscience. *I feel a peace about doing this.*

"If you feel such peace about it, why are you arguing with me?"

Good question. I didn't have an answer, so I decided to try the silent method and ignore him. I kept picturing Jiminy Cricket hounding Pinocchio. If my conscience had been a cricket at that moment, I probably would have squashed him.

I just didn't want to deal with it. Good grief, Shannon and I were already very, very pure physically. We'd made the commitment not to kiss till our wedding day. The most we did as an *engaged* couple was hold hands or put our arms around each other. So yes, we were lying in a hammock together. So what? Yes, our bodies were rather close. Yes, we were sort of wedged up against each other. And yes, it was sensual, and it was turning me on. But darn it, I would not be ruled by legalism!

"Stop looking at her legs, Josh," my conscience said. "Your half-open eyelids don't fool me."

I'm just admiring them.

"You're lusting."

Well, she is going to be my wife in four months.

"Well, she's not your wife today."

God does not want me to stifle my sexuality!

"Stifle, no. Control for the sake of righteousness, yes."

Why does everything have to be such a big deal?

"Let me ask you one more question, and then I'll leave you alone."

What?

"If Jesus Christ—the one who blessed you with your sexuality and brought this girl into your life, the one who sacrificed His life to redeem you and set you apart for holiness—if *He* were to walk up and lay His nail-scarred hand on this hammock, would you be proud of what you're doing?"

I was silent.

"Josh?"

I'm getting out.

I swung my legs over the side of the hammock and tumbled out.

"Something wrong?" Shannon asked, startled by my sudden departure.

"I shouldn't be in this with you," I said. "I'm sorry, but I'm enjoying this for the wrong reasons. I'm sorry I suggested it. I need to take a walk."

"Okay," she said and smiled. She was unaware of the

heated debate that had been raging at the other end of the hammock. "I love you," she called after me.

"I love you, too," I said. I really did love her. And that's why I walked away.

Not Just Waiting Around

"Among you," God tells His children, "there must not be even a hint of sexual immorality, or of any kind of impurity" (Ephesians 5:3). It's because of clear commands like this and the reality of our God-given sexual appetites that we face "hammock" moments—moments when we must choose between what our bodies crave and what we know our Lord has instructed.

The temptation may be as seemingly innocent as deciding when to kiss, or as serious as choosing when to sleep together. Whatever it is, the internal struggle is the same. The question boils down to, Whom will you believe? Will you heed the clear commands of Scripture and the voice of your conscience, or the voice of compromise that's offering immediate pleasure? What's *really* going to make you happy?

We all know how we're *supposed* to answer, but when our desire kicks in, doing what's right isn't easy. In the heat of passion, we need more than just knowledge about sexual purity. To stand firm against sin, we can't simply intellectually agree with the merits of chastity. We must be *captivated* by the beauty and greater pleasure of God's way. This involves *agreeing* with God about the goodness of pure sex within marriage, *refusing* the counterfeits offered by the world, and *fearing* the consequences of illicit sex.

Being captivated by God's way won't happen by accident—it requires purposeful effort before marriage. Author Ken Myers once told me, "True love doesn't *just* wait; it plans." He's right. While we're single or in a courtship, we need to do more than just avoid what's wrong—we need to plan and work hard at being captivated by the good. In this chapter we're going to look at how during courtship and engagement you can be planning for a thrilling, God-glorifying sex life in marriage. Are you ready to be captivated?

Worship in Bed

God celebrates pure sex within marriage. He invites us to do the same. "What more divine gift of celebration do we have than lovemaking?" asks Douglas Jones. He writes that the marriage bed should not "merely be a place of satisfying natural urges, but a place for delighting in the mysterious beauty of those drives. Why did God delight to entrance us with smooth skin, soft breasts, firm muscles, entangled legs, and slow kisses?"

Why did God delight to make us so? The answer is for our enjoyment and His glory. Because He's very, very good. He could have made the means by which we procreate as brief and boring as sneezing. Instead, He gave it more sizzle than the Fourth of July. And when a husband and wife revel in and thank God for the gift of sex, they glorify Him. Their lovemaking becomes a jubilant, two-person worship service!

To plan ahead for a great sex life, we have to realize that the message of Scripture is not for us to disdain sex, but to love God's original design so much that we see the world's perversions of it as revolting. "Enjoy pure sex!" God practically shouts in Proverbs 5:18–19: "May your fountain be blessed, and may you rejoice in the wife of your youth.... May her breasts satisfy you always, may you ever be captivated by her love."

There's that word again—*captivated*. It means to be amazed and taken prisoner by the beauty of something. "Be captivated, be ravished by the body of your spouse," God tells us. "Be entranced by the true and lasting pleasure of the marriage bed."

Ensnared by Illicit Sex

Only when we're captivated by the goodness of God's plan can we avoid becoming prisoners to immorality. We can either be captives of righteousness or captives of sin. "The evil deeds of a wicked man ensnare him; the cords of his sin hold him fast" (Proverbs 5:22). The man and woman who embrace the immediate pleasure of sex outside of marriage may think that they are experiencing freedom, but the opposite is true—the tentacles of sin are reaching up, binding them, and dragging them toward death.

What will we choose? God urges us to choose life and true pleasure:

> Drink water from your own well—share your love only with your wife. Why spill the water of your springs in public, having sex with just anyone? You should reserve it for yourselves. Don't share it with strangers. Why be captivated, my son, with an

immoral woman, or embrace the breasts of an adulterous woman? (Proverbs 5:15–17, 20, NLT)

Scripture doesn't deny the pleasure of illicit sex—yes, it will feel good; yes, it can be exciting. But its pleasure is empty compared to the joys of married love and foolish in light of the dire consequences that visit soul, body, and emotions. "Within marriage, sex is beautiful, fulfilling, creative," writes John MacArthur. "Outside of marriage, it is ugly, destructive and damning."

What's the payoff of sexual sin? "You will lose your honor and hand over to merciless people everything you have achieved in life. Strangers will obtain your wealth, and someone else will enjoy the fruit of your labor. Afterward you will groan in anguish when disease consumes your body" (Proverbs 5:9–11, NLT).

Is the Bible exaggerating? No, it's not. Ask Michelle, a girl I met at a Christian bookstore in Phoenix. For twenty-two years she saved her virginity for her future husband. She was working as a model when she met an attractive man who was determined to deflower her. She toyed with him, loving the attention. Then one day on his apartment couch she gave in to his advances. Only once. Less than an hour of stolen pleasure. Now he's gone, and she's a single mom struggling to care for her fatherless two-year-old daughter.

The Bible isn't just being dramatic when it says that you'll "groan in anguish when disease consumes your body." Just ask the missionary in Asia that a pastor told me about. He was a virgin in his early thirties and two months away from getting married. One night, inflamed by lust and tired of resisting temptation, he made his way to the red-light district of the city and the bed of a prostitute. Only once. Just fifteen minutes in a dark, dingy room—a moment of indulgence in years of work for God. But he left infected with AIDS. Two months later he unwittingly infected the bride who had waited so patiently for him. He groans in anguish at the disease that now wracks both of their bodies.

If these examples seem extreme, just look into the eyes of the countless men and women who have neither illegitimate children nor disease, but who are scarred with shame and regret. Writer Deborah Belonick knows too many women who once "regarded sexual liberation as good, clean fun," but who are now reaping bitter results. She describes women who, now married with children, "could not have their husbands touch them or hold them in certain ways because it reminded them of drunken orgies they'd participated in in college or high school. Women who were infertile due to damage from sexually transmitted disease. Women who had to undergo biopsies for precancerous conditions due to too many sexual partners." Ask women like these if it was worth it. Talk to the married couples who sinned together before marriage and who have spent years recovering from the bitterness and distrust it sowed in their relationship.

And if all this isn't enough to make the option of sexual immorality vile, look into the eyes of Jesus Christ. He's the only one who knows the depth of God's unmitigated wrath against sexual sin—He bore it all when He hung on the cross, cursed and forsaken by His Father (2 Corinthians 5:21; Galatians 3:13).

No Excuses

Part of the motivation we need in order to hold out for the pleasure of pure sex is a sober acknowledgment that God is serious about punishing sin. Let's not kid ourselves. God is talking to *us*. "God will judge the adulterer and all the sexually immoral" (Hebrews 13:4). And in 1 Thessalonians 4:6, we read, "The Lord will punish men for all such sins, as we have already told you and warned you." We can't be flippant about this. It has to sink in.

God doesn't excuse sin because of who we are or how good we've been in the past. It doesn't matter if you've lived a sexually pure life for forty years and then have one night of sin—God still hates that act of fornication. Read the story of King David's adulterous affair with Bathsheba in 2 Samuel 11. Even though God called David "a man after his own heart" (1 Samuel 13:14), He hated David's sin and He punished it. David was forgiven when he repented, but the consequences of his sin marred the remainder of his life. The lesson for us is that God's righteous standard will not be relaxed for *anyone*.

God doesn't overlook our sin because it's not as bad as someone else's. We can always find someone else or some other couple who are more disobedient than we are, but that doesn't change the reality of our own disobedience. God doesn't grade on a curve. He doesn't base His judgments on the popular standards of the day—His standards are unchanging (Psalm 102:27; Hebrews 13:8).

God doesn't excuse our sin because we're in love and "no one is being hurt." You've heard the argument; maybe you've even used it yourself: "We're two consenting adults. We love each other! We both want this!" But do you see who's being forgotten in the equation of "two consenting adults"? The almighty Creator of their two bodies.

The apostle Paul explains:

> In sexual sin we violate the sacredness of our own bodies, these bodies that were made for God-given and God-modeled love, for "becoming one" with another. Or didn't you realize that your body is a sacred place, the place of the Holy Spirit? Don't you see that you can't live however you please, squandering what God paid such a high price for? (1 Corinthians 6:18–20, *The Message*)

The warnings are serious and there are no exceptions. Sure, some people seemingly escape them, but there will be a reckoning beyond this life—"they will have to give account to him who is ready to judge the living and the dead" (1 Peter 4:5). Every man and woman who refuses to turn from sexual sin and trust in Christ for forgiveness will one day look into the eyes of a Holy Judge—the short-lived pleasure of sin will be forgotten, and it will be too late for mercy.

Why Your Sex Drive Is a Blessing

"Okay," you're thinking, "I agree that sex in marriage sounds great, and I believe that sexual sin leads to death. But none of this deals with my raging sex desire right now! Did God make me like this just to torment me?"

No, He did not. Even though our sexual desire can seem like a curse, and even though we have to restrain it for our own good, we need to keep in mind that these desires are natural, God given, and wonderful. In fact, they're a blessing even when we can't satisfy them.

Let me explain what I mean. If God had made sex so undesirable that we were never tempted to steal it before marriage, it wouldn't be much of a gift, would it? Every time we long for sexual intimacy before marriage, we should quickly thank God for making us sexual beings and for making sex so desirable. The Bible says, "Guard the sacredness of sexual intimacy between wife and husband" (Hebrews 13:4, *The Message*). It's because God has made sex a precious treasure that He's commanded us to guard it.

And not only did God make sex good, but He also increased our enjoyment by reserving it for marriage. If we didn't have to wait for it, there'd be no anticipation, no buildup, no excitement.

When I was young, I read the story of a boy who was granted his wish that every day would be Christmas. For a while it was paradise—every morning he dashed downstairs to newly stuffed stockings and dozens of presents under the tree. But in a very short time, the celebration lost its joy. There was no longer anything special about it. He began to despise the presents. He had thought that he would find happiness in boundless Christmases but instead he gutted the holiday of its meaning and pleasure.

Couples who impatiently and greedily take sex outside the boundaries of marriage do the same thing. It's like Christmas every day. The act loses its beauty and uniqueness.

They end up cheating themselves out of sex at its best.

Why does God ask single Christians to face the daily struggle of controlling their sexual appetites until marriage? One answer is that He's committed to great sex! I've read that honeymoon resorts are having to provide more and more activities for newlyweds who, since they didn't wait, are bored with sex by the time they get married. While many sexually promiscuous couples greet the marriage bed with a yawn, the chaste fall into it with cries of delight. On our honeymoon, Shannon and I didn't need a schedule packed with activities. We rarely left our hotel room! We had stored up passion; we were full of anticipation and pure desire. Everything was new, fresh, and intoxicating.

There's another reason the struggle of waiting for marriage is a blessing. God not only wants to maximize a couple's enjoyment of sex in marriage, He also wants them to learn to trust Him *together.* When a Christian man and woman systematically deny their own physical desires as an expression of mutual faith and submission to Jesus Christ, they are laying a solid spiritual foundation for their marriage. They're learning to fight sin as a team. They're learning to care for each other, pray for each other, and challenge each other. In the most practical of ways, they are submitting to Jesus Christ as the Lord of their relationship.

Demonstrating the Depth of Your Love

Far from being a curse, God's call to chastity is a blessing. Of course it rarely feels like one, and when we're in the thick of it, it's never easy. That's why it's so important that we have a clear game plan for our physical relationship. We need principles that will help us align our hearts and our actions with God's plan. Remember, our goal is to be captivated by God's plan for pure sex. The motive for our self-control and restraint is not asceticism or religious piety, but joy, true pleasure, and God's glory.

Let me share a few of the principles that helped Shannon and me during our courtship and engagement. The first is this:

1. During courtship, guarding each other's purity and refraining from sexual intimacy are the acts of lovemaking.

A Christian man and woman in love have to redefine what true lovemaking is before they're married. They have to agree that sexual intimacy before marriage is most *unloving*. They have to renew their thinking so that they both see that not violating their future marriage bed is a true expression of love.

Do you want to be romantic with the person you're courting? Do you want to demonstrate your passion for them with more than words? Then guard against sin, fight lust, and refuse to arouse them sexually—this is the only God-sanctioned form of lovemaking in courtship and engagement.

I opened this chapter with the story of my temptation in the hammock. Walking away from Shannon that summer day was the real way for me to demonstrate my love for her. I wasn't denying the reality of my love or my sexual desire for her; I was increasing it and purifying it by submitting it to God. She appreciated that. Even though there was part of her heart that wanted me to stay, she felt my love for her as I turned my back on temptation.

"This is how we know what love is: Jesus Christ laid down his life for us. And we ought to lay down our lives for our brothers" (1 John 3:16). Before marriage, two friends who are not yet lovers can prove their love by laying down their own sexual desires and protecting each other's purity.

Learning to Recognize True Affection

Learning to recognize true affection can be difficult, especially if you've learned to equate sex with love. Sonya was three when her father left her mom. She grew up searching for love in the arms of different boyfriends. She never found it because she mistook physical involvement for true affection. After becoming a Christian, she brought her old perceptions into her relationship with Zachary. Though Zachary deeply cared about her, she began doubting it because he hadn't tried to sleep with her. "It was really twisted thinking," she says. "I'd finally found a guy who really loved me, and I didn't feel his love because he hadn't tried to use me like all my old boyfriends had."

It took lots of communication, prayer, and humble leadership on Zachary's part to help Sonya change her thinking. She came to see that the absence of a physical relationship was not a lack of love, but a sign of it. She also had to work through the deeply rooted pattern of looking to men instead of to her heavenly Father for comfort and confidence.

It's important in your relationship that neither of you try

to test each other's convictions or tempt the other person to violate his or her standards.

Brad continually tried to wear down his girlfriend, Allison, with requests for "just one kiss," even though they had agreed to save that for engagement. We should never expect the other person to be the strong one and force them to bear the weight of temptation. How unloving! Before marriage true love is expressed through guarding and refraining.

Don't Try to Bargain

An essential part of planning for pure sex in courtship and engagement is understanding the lie of lust. The following principle can give you an edge against it:

2. Lust is never satisfied.

Lust would like us to believe that it can make us happy, that if we'll just give it what it wants, it will stop pestering us and be satisfied. Don't buy it. Lust is never satisfied. You can't bargain with it and come out a winner. Lust hijacks sex. It wants to train your desires to delight in the thrill of the forbidden so that you lose your godly appetite for what is good.

Ray and Angelina slept with each other during their nine-month engagement. It felt so right, how could it be wrong? "It was incredible. There was this animal passion between us," Ray says. They justified their fornication by saying that their "electric" sex confirmed that they were supposed to be married. And they assumed that the extra practice in bed would only benefit them in the future. They were wrong. They bargained with lust, and they got ripped off.

A year and a half after their wedding, the sizzle had vanished from their sex life. Sadly, they went back to the bargaining table with lust. They started renting pornographic movies to "enhance" their passion. It didn't work. The more inflamed they became with lust, the less satisfied they felt. Now Ray is starting to view pornography on the Internet and cast a longing eye at women at work. Once again lust is telling him that "what he really needs" is something that he doesn't have.

Is Ray and Angelina's story proof that marriage ruins sex? No, it's another sad example of *lust* ruining sex. During their engagement they learned to delight in what was off-limits. They weren't being driven by a passion for the goodness of pure sex; their passion was fueled by the sinful thrill of lust. When they got married and sex became something good and pure, they had no appetite for it.

Don't try to bargain with lust. Kill it. Don't spend the season of courtship giving in to it—in your mind or your actions—and learning to delight in sin instead of righteousness. Once you do, you'll never find true satisfaction. For more help in battling lust I've written the book *Sex Is Not the Problem (Lust Is)* for men and women who desire sexual purity.

When Fantasy Goes Too Far

It's tempting during courtship, and especially during engagement, to begin to fantasize about making love with your future spouse. Be careful that joyful, God-centered anticipation doesn't turn into unbridled lust. Even though it's not easy, you still need to guard your heart. It's never right to fantasize about sexual immorality, and it's very easy to go from "imagining the wedding night" to sinful fantasy.

During our engagement, I struggled the most with sexual thoughts about Shannon in the morning. It always happened right when I woke up. If I allowed myself to lie in bed for an extra five minutes and dream about how one day I'd be waking up next to her, lust often got the better of me—if not at the moment, then later in how I treated her when we were together. In spite of failing often, by God's grace I was committed to fighting lust. I knew that the moment I stopped struggling against my sinful nature and started believing the lies of lust, I'd be lost.

That's why I jumped out of bed and cried out to God for grace in my times of weakness. That's why I was accountable to my roommate, Andrew, and my pastor about my thought life. That's why, when sexual thoughts about Shannon came, I did my best to turn my focus to thanking God for what our future held and to asking for His help to be patient and strong in the meantime.

Yellow Lines

The reality of indwelling sin and the deceit of lust is why this next principle is so important. To fight and avoid sexual sin, we need a game plan. This principle helps us connect our convictions to our actions:

3. Specific guidelines for your physical relationship can never replace humble reliance on the Holy Spirit—but they can reinforce your biblical convictions.

Every couple needs to search Scripture and come up with their own specific guidelines for what they will and won't do in their physical relationship. These guidelines should never become a replacement for prayer and constant reliance on the Holy Spirit. Instead, they should be seen as an expression of a sincere desire to please and obey God. A vague definition of righteousness quickly leads to compromise.

The guidelines that you and your boyfriend or girlfriend come up with are like the yellow lines that divide a road. Can they stop you from sinning? No. Do they negate the importance of carefully evaluating your heart and your motives? Not at all. But they're still important. We need the yellow lines on a road even though they can't stop a car from swerving into the wrong lane and having a head-on collision. Though the lines are unable to stop a driver who wants to ignore them, they do help drivers who want to avoid danger.

Here is what's important to understand: We can't *start* by making our guidelines. Our starting point has to be a heart desire to honor God with our bodies and to serve each other. Paul was right when he said that rules for the sake of rules and rules that originate from human traditions and glorify human piety have no "value in restraining sensual indulgence" (Colossians 2:23). Only the power of the Holy Spirit working in us can change us. Only by His grace can we learn to say no to ungodliness (Titus 2:12).

But here's where many people misunderstand and misapply this passage. An important part of receiving and applying God's grace in our lives is establishing behavior that flees from temptation and puts sin to death. This involves establishing guidelines—yes, rules—that help us. These rules aren't our hope, they don't earn God's love, and they aren't our starting point; but they can help us put our convictions into action.

Our Guidelines

After our "nap" in the hammock, I realized that Shannon and I needed stricter and more specific guidelines for our physical relationship. We were accountable to friends, but we hadn't really spelled out what it meant for us to be obedient. It was all subjective. "How are you two doing lately?" my parents would ask. "Uh, I think we're doing pretty good…I guess," I'd say, trying to remember if I felt guilty about anything that had occurred recently. As I looked ahead to the four months before our wedding, I knew it would only get more difficult to stick to our convictions.

Let me tell you some of the guidelines we came up with. In sharing them, I'm not saying that you should follow them. You have to develop your own convictions and guidelines from Scripture. You'll have different strengths and weaknesses. What I want to illustrate is how important it is to be *specific*.

We will not caress each other. For us this excludes:

- rubbing each other's back, neck, or arms;
- touching or stroking each other's face;
- playing with each other's hair;
- scratching each other's arms or back.

We will not "cuddle." For us this excludes:

- sitting entwined on a couch watching a movie;
- leaning or resting on the other person;
- lying down next to each other;
- playfully wrestling with each other.

We will guard our conversation and meditation. For us this means:

- not talking about our future physical relationship;
- not thinking or dwelling on what would now be sinful;
- not reading things related to physical intimacy within marriage prematurely.

We will not spend undue amounts of time together at late hours.

A specific area of concern for us is time together late at night. We're more vulnerable when we're tired. Even if we haven't compromised, please ask if we're spending too much time together at late hours.

Appropriate physical expressions during this season include:

- holding hands;
- Josh putting his arm around Shannon's shoulder;
- brief "side hugs."

These guidelines are "fences" to keep us far from violating God's commands.

Our greatest concern is the direction and intention of our hearts. Even if we're following them to the smallest detail, please inquire if any action or activity is stirring up inappropriate desire or awakening love before its time.

Looking at these guidelines now, I smile. They are extremely detailed. But at that unique season in our relationship, that is what we needed to stand by our convictions. Even though it was embarrassing, we gave a copy of these guidelines to my parents, my pastor and his wife, another married couple we were close to, my best friend, and Shannon's three roommates. We didn't want any safe havens for compromise. We wanted everyone in our lives to know our standards and to help us stick to them. They did. Shannon's roommates had our guidelines posted on their refrigerator!

Let me say it again: My goal in sharing our guidelines is not that you'll adopt them. You might be able to do some of these things with a clear conscience before God. Whatever guidelines you come up with need to grow out of the clear teaching of Scripture and from sincere conviction so you can follow them with joy.

I encourage you to take the time to "paint the yellow lines" for your relationship. You don't need them when you're feeling strong and spiritually sharp—you need them for the moments when your resistance is weak and your sense of conviction dull. In those moments of weakness you don't want to start having to decide what you should and shouldn't do. If you make your choices then, you'll wind up in compromise.

The Big Deal About Little Things

So how should *you* decide what you do or don't do in your physical relationship before marriage? This next principle can help you formulate your own guidelines:

4. The longer your "no big deal" list is before marriage, the shorter your "very special" list will be after marriage.

This principle reminds us that we should base our decisions of what we do and don't do in our physical relationship on a desire to maximize the joy and pleasure of sex within marriage.

Many couples spend much of the dating and courtship phases convincing themselves that things like kissing and sexual touching are "no big deal." When they finally reach the marriage bed, there's very little left that can be considered unique and special to marriage. They're the ones to lose!

I've already mentioned that Shannon and I decided to save our first kiss for our wedding day. This is another example of an outward action that is meaningless unless it's backed up by a heart desire to glorify God and serve each other. I don't encourage couples to make this or any other commitment so they can feel morally superior to other people. Neither do I think that this should be the litmus test of truly godly relationships. As you've already heard, I sinned more in my heart without kissing

Shannon than many guys who kiss their girlfriends. The most important issue is our motive and our heart before God.

But let me share why Shannon and I decided to make kissing a "big deal." First, we had both been in previous relationships in which we kissed other people. We knew how meaningless this could be apart from true love. We wanted to "redeem" kissing, if you will, and make it a privilege of marriage. Second, we understood the progressive nature of sexual involvement. Once you start kissing, you want to move on. We didn't want to start what we couldn't finish. When a man and woman's lips meet, and their tongues penetrate each other's mouths, their process of becoming one has begun.

It's a Package

Another way to put it is that we viewed kissing as part of the whole package of sexual union. And we didn't want to dissect the sex act into stages so we could justify enjoying more and more of lovemaking outside of marriage.

Many Christian couples have the conviction that sex should be saved for marriage. Unfortunately, all this really means is that they're saving intercourse for marriage. Do you see how ludicrous this is? Sex is so much more than just penetration. As John White puts it, "Defining coitus in terms of penetration and orgasm has as much moral significance and as much logical difficulty as trying to define a beard by the number of hairs on a chin." He goes on to reveal just how silly it is to try to break the passion of lovemaking into stages:

I know that experts used to distinguish light from heavy petting, and heavy petting from intercourse, but is there any moral difference between two naked people in bed petting to orgasm and another two having intercourse? Is the one act a fraction of an ounce less sinful than the other?

Is it perhaps more righteous to pet with clothes on? If so, which is worse, to pet with clothes off or to have intercourse with clothes on?

You may accuse me of being crude. Far from it. If we pursue the argument far enough, we will see that an approach to the morality of premarital sex that is based on the details of behavior (kissing, dressing or undressing, touching, holding, looking) and parts of the body (fingers, hair, arms, breasts, lips, genitalia) can satisfy only a Pharisee. A look can be as sensual as touch, and a finger brushed lightly over a cheek as erotic as penetration.

In an insightful article entitled "(Don't) Kiss Me," Bethany Torode points out that the problem among many Christians is that we "don't acknowledge sexual intimacy as a whole package." Bethany shares her own convictions about kissing and challenges Christians to take time to consider the deeper significance of something many of us have learned to treat nonchalantly. She writes:

I'm a sophomore in college with virgin lips. A few months after turning 16, I vowed to keep my "bow" tied until a man promises to commit himself to the whole package. My first kiss will be from my husband on our wedding day. Yes, that's quite a progression, from an inexpert kiss at the altar to the complete unwrapping of the wedding night—believe me, my friends have pointed that out. Then again, Adam and Eve managed to figure everything out.

What Bethany and many other Christians are realizing is that when it comes to a physical relationship, "the beginning and the ending of passion are inseparable." We're the ones who lose when we make any other form of physical intimacy "no big deal." Even our kissing should be informed by an overriding desire to glorify God and to be captivated by sex within marriage. Bethany continues:

God never intended the engagement period to be a time for physical experimenting, for peeking under the wrapping paper. Kissing—which quickly turns passionate when you are in love—carries a current intended to light a fire. In the Old Testament, the Hebrew word for kiss (*nashaq*) is derived from the primary root meaning "to kindle." I don't want to open the matchbox.

We see this truth reflected in writings from Scripture to literature that has endured for centuries. Song of Solomon 8:4 says not to arouse love until the right time. The fairy tales *Sleeping Beauty* and *Snow White* have deep symbolic meaning: A kiss is (and should be) an awakening. I want to guard my fiancé; I want him to be asleep to me until we are one before

God. There are other ways of showing affection without arousing passion.

Can you kiss to the glory of God before marriage? I'm sure there are many couples who can. But if you realize you can't, be willing to refrain. Ask yourself, "Why is it so important to me that we be kissing now? Is my sinful heart deceiving me? Am I being motivated by lust?" The thing that matters is our motive and the fruit of our actions.

Even Porn Stars Draw Lines

I encourage you to make as many parts of your physical relationship as you can precious and treasured parts of marriage. I once read a newspaper article that quoted a woman who had starred in many pornographic movies. Surprisingly, this woman had stipulated in her contract that she would never have to kiss the male actors with whom she had sex before the cameras. Why would a woman who gives her body to every form of sexual perversion care about a kiss? The answer she gave was that a kiss was one of the few remaining intimate and precious things she could reserve for her boyfriend.

I wanted to cry when I read that. I thought of all the men and women who have been shocked, even offended, by my decision not to kiss my wife until we were married. "Kissing is no big deal!" I've heard over and over. So who's right? Are they, or is the porn star? I believe that they're both wrong. We can't make certain parts of sexual intimacy meaningful and others meaningless—it's *all* precious! It's as ridiculous to say, "It's just a kiss!" as it is to say, "It's just intercourse!" They're both part of the amazing and mysterious gift of sex, which God created so that husbands and wives can become "one flesh." Let's treat it all as precious!

Good in Bed

The fear that many people have about not having a physical relationship before marriage is that they'll be clumsy and inexperienced on their wedding night. Guess what? It's okay to be clumsy and inexperienced. It means you need to devote a lot of time to practice after the wedding.

I received an e-mail from a girl named Rita who was very concerned about my decision not to kiss Shannon until we were married. She had talked to a friend who said that without *some* form of physical interaction before marriage, there could be damaging effects on our sex life. Shannon would feel like she was being raped, and I might not be able to turn my sex drive on after having controlled it for so long. (Neither was a problem, by the way.)

I answered Rita by saying that the transition a couple makes between no physical contact and full consummation *is* important, but that it should take place *after* marriage, not before it. There's no rule that says newlyweds have to have sex their first night together. They can warm up slowly. They can take as long as they need to get used to kissing and touching each other. They can grow accustomed to being naked together. They don't have to have intercourse immediately. (Though I've met few couples who had trouble feeling ready very quickly.)

The point is that the focus for both people (especially the

man) should be on serving the other person, not demanding gratification. Part of the beauty of a Christian marriage between two partners who have not known each other sexually is the discovery and mutual learning experience. "I don't plan to be an 'expert in bed' when I get married," I told the girl who had written me. And that shouldn't be anyone's goal. Our main concern as Christians should be purity before God, not being experienced lovers when we get married.

The world has turned sex into a sport to be scored and evaluated like figure skating. What it lacks in true love, it replaces with an obsession over performance. What a sad replacement! Who cares if you or your partner can have the "ultimate orgasm" if neither of you truly care about each other?

One of the best gifts you can give your future husband or wife is the assurance that they don't have to be experts on the wedding night. What a wonderful opportunity you both have to trust God together—to say to Him, "Lord, we believe that You are good and that Your plan for sex is the best. We trust You so much we're willing to show up on our wedding night as novices. No practice, no experience, just a desire to learn and to rejoice in the new discoveries we'll make."

But will we be compatible? If you love each other and you're willing to learn and gently respond to the desires of your lover, yes, you will be. Only selfishness and sin make two people sexually incompatible.

The Best Wedding Gifts

True love plans. Do you really care for each other? Then spend your courtship storing up passion and planning for thrilling, God-glorifying sex. The most important thing you can do during this time is to learn to think biblically about sex, to love God's plan, and to battle the lust and impatience in you that will try to destroy it.

The effort will be more than worth it. Each time you feel as though you're *denying* yourselves, you're actually *blessing* yourselves. Each time you walk away from temptation and refuse to stoke the fires of passion prematurely, you're sending yourselves the best gifts you'll receive on the day of your wedding—gifts of trust and respect and increased passion.

part 3

———

BEFORE YOU
SAY "I DO"

Chapter Ten

WHEN YOUR PAST COMES KNOCKING

How You Can Face Past Sexual Sin and Experience God's Forgiveness

The past. Strange, isn't it? So much of what you want to remember fades like a dream. But what you *don't* want to remember? That can hang on for a lifetime. The memories and guilt of past sin chase you. Just when it seems that you've outrun them, they come knocking at your door—to remind, to taunt, to condemn.

The past knocked on Shannon's door almost as soon as we started our relationship. Though she had lived a chaste life since becoming a Christian three years earlier, she had many regrets about choices she had made before her conversion. She had lost her virginity when she was fourteen. Throughout high school and college she was rarely without a boyfriend. She lived for the pleasure of the moment. She was careless, even reckless.

No one tells you about the pain and regret at the end of it all, she often thought. If only she'd known the consequences of her choices. If only she'd known how irretrievable lost innocence is.

Now the moment she had dreaded was upon her. She had to look me in the eyes and speak the words she knew would pierce me. "Please prepare Josh's heart for what I need to tell him," she pleaded to God in her journal. "Lord, if he decides he can't take me as his wife, help me to remember that You are my rock and my comfort. My past belongs to You."

Her eyes were filled with sadness the night she informed me that we needed to talk about what she described as "bad stuff." "Can we talk now?" I asked.

"No," she said. "Let's wait till tomorrow."

I picked her up the next evening, and we drove to an off-beat restaurant in Bethesda called Thyme Square. Brightly colored vegetables were painted on the walls; the bread was served in flower pots. On any other night we would have enjoyed the unique surroundings, but that night our hearts were heavy.

"I want you to know," she began, "that if you decide you need to end our relationship after you hear what I have to say, I won't hold it against you."

"Shannon—"

"No, I mean that," she said. A tear dripped off her nose. We were both quiet. The food arrived, but we hardly noticed. When the server came back to check on us, she raised her eyebrows at our untouched plates, and then, sensing our need for privacy, turned away.

Shannon's tear-soaked napkin lay crumpled on the table

in front of her. She opened her mouth to try again, but faltered and dropped her head. She just couldn't get it out. The task was too hard. The words were unbearably heavy, and she felt so weak.

"I'm sorry," she whispered.

"It's all right," I said. "There's no rush."

The Saddest and the Happiest

We took our time that evening. The words eventually came. When Shannon told me that she wasn't a virgin, I assured her that it didn't change my feelings for her. I told her that although I had never had sex, I'd compromised my purity with girls in the past. I asked for her forgiveness too. We both shed tears.

The conversation was the beginning of a difficult journey of faith for us. Yet through it all, God sustained and guided us. If you're facing similar circumstances, I know that He can do the same for you.

Though it's painful, an important part of starting a new life with the person you love is working through the consequences of past choices. This doesn't mean that you have to dredge up every sordid detail, but it does mean that you need to honestly face the effect your past can have on your future. As the authors of *Preparing for Marriage* wisely state, "It is better to speak the truth prior to your marriage than to live with the fear, deceit, and shame that comes from hiding the truth from your mate."

Unless you are honest about past sin, you won't be able to understand the potential challenges you'll confront because of it. Neither will you be able to root yourselves firmly in the sustaining grace of God.

This chapter is about how Jesus' death on the cross enables us to face our past. It will help you to know God's forgiveness *personally* and to *extend* forgiveness to another.

So while in some ways this chapter is the saddest in this book, it's also the happiest. It deals with the heartbreaking effects of sin; but more important, it magnifies the love of our redeeming God—a God whose grace is *greater* than anything from our past. Although the following pages may bring up painful memories, my goal is to make you more aware of God's grace than you are of your own sin.

Why the Cross?

"Have I spoiled God's perfect plan for me?" nineteen-year-old Blaire asked in a handwritten note. After a difficult breakup, she had grown bitter toward God and rebelled against Him by sleeping with a guy she hardly knew. Now she was anguishing in the aftermath of her fornication. She had dashed her dream of being a virgin on her wedding night—she had robbed her future husband. Would any godly man want her now?

"I gave myself to someone I didn't even love!" she wrote. "Does God still want me in His kingdom? How can He use someone who is so impure? Does He still love me, even though I turned my back on Him, my family, and everything I was raised to believe? Is it too late for me?"

Can you relate to Blaire's question? Do you carry regret over sin you've committed? Do you ever wonder whether

God can really forgive? And if He does, is it really sincere? Or will He always view you suspiciously? Are you on lifelong probation? Is God holding your past sin over you, ready to rain down judgment at the slightest mistake?

"I repented, and I know the Bible says that I'm forgiven," a guy named Tony told me. "But sometimes I think God is keeping me single to punish me for my sexual sin back in college. Every time a friend gets married, I feel like He's rubbing my face in it."

Is this how God works? *No, it's not.*

Is God's forgiveness halfhearted? *No, it isn't.*

Are people who have sinned sexually forever condemned to second-class status in God's family? *Absolutely not!*

Many Christians believe these lies and live in condemnation because they base their understanding of forgiveness on a faulty understanding of who God is. The greatest hindrance to knowing God's forgiveness is ignorance about Him. If our knowledge of God's character is unclear and vague, our confidence in His forgiveness will be too.

The truth is that it's not too late for *anyone* who's ready to repent to be forgiven (1 John 1:9). God is in the business of making people new (2 Corinthians 5:17). He wants to give you "hope and a future" (Jeremiah 29:11). He wants you to be absolutely sure of His love for you. And that's why He bids you come and gaze on the Cross.

The Great Rescue

What does Jesus' death have to do with working through past sexual sin? How can a gruesome crucifixion that happened

two thousand years ago help when your past comes knocking *today?*

The answer is that the Cross is *God's* plan for freeing you
from the guilt and punishment of your past sin. At the Cross
we see both the depths of our depravity and the heights of
God's amazing love for us. We witness both the terrifying
intensity of God's just wrath for sin and His unspeakable
mercy and love for sinners.

Why the Cross?

Because sinners have no other hope.

Why the Cross?

Because it is the unassailable proof that we *can* be forgiven.

Let's gaze on it together. As we draw close, don't assume
that you already know or understand what happened there.
Come to the Cross as if for the first time. In the book *When
God Weeps,* Steven Estes and Joni Eareckson Tada give the
following account of Christ's death. As you read, refuse to
let the scene be familiar. Let its reality shock you and break
your heart.

The face that Moses had begged to see—was forbidden to see—was slapped bloody (Exodus 33:19–20).
The thorns that God had sent to curse the earth's
rebellion now twisted around his own brow....

"On your back with you!" One raises a mallet to
sink in the spike. But the soldier's heart must continue pumping as he readies the prisoner's wrist.
Someone must sustain the soldier's life minute by
minute, for no man has this power on his own. Who
supplies breath to his lungs? Who gives energy to

his cells? Who holds his molecules together? Only by the Son do "all things hold together" (Colossians 1:17). The victim wills that the soldier live on—he grants the warriors continued existence. The man swings.

As the man swings, the Son recalls how he and the Father first designed the medial nerve of the human forearm—the sensations it would be capable of. The design proves flawless—the nerves perform exquisitely. "Up you go!" They lift the cross. God is on display in his underwear and can scarcely breathe.

But these pains are a mere warm-up to his other and growing dread. He begins to feel a foreign sensation. Somewhere during this day an unearthly foul odor began to waft, not around his nose, but his heart. He *feels* dirty. Human wickedness starts to crawl upon his spotless being—the living excrement from our souls. The apple of his Father's eye turns brown with rot.

His Father! He must face his Father like this!

From heaven the Father now rouses himself like a lion disturbed, shakes his mane, and roars against the shriveling remnant of a man hanging on a cross. Never has the Son seen the Father look at him so, never felt even the least of his hot breath. But the roar shakes the unseen world and darkens the visible sky. The Son does not recognize these eyes.

"Son of Man! Why have you behaved so? You have cheated, lusted, stolen, gossiped—murdered, envied, hated, lied. You have cursed, robbed, overspent, overeaten—fornicated, disobeyed, embezzled, and blasphemed. Oh, the duties you have shirked, the children you have abandoned! Who has ever so ignored the poor, so played the coward, so belittled my name? Have you *ever* held your razor tongue? What a self-righteous, pitiful drunk—*you,* who molest young boys, peddle killer drugs, travel in cliques, and mock your parents. Who gave you the boldness to rig elections, foment revolutions, torture animals, and worship demons? Does the list never end! Splitting families, raping virgins, acting smugly, playing the pimp—buying politicians, practicing exhortation, filming pornography, accepting bribes. You have burned down buildings, perfected terrorist tactics, founded false religions, traded in slaves—relishing each morsel and bragging about it all. I hate, *loathe* these things in you! Disgust for everything about you consumes me! Can you not feel my wrath?"

Of course the Son is innocent. He is blamelessness itself. The Father knows this. But the divine pair have an agreement, and the unthinkable must now take place. Jesus will be treated as if personally responsible for every sin ever committed.

The Father watches as his heart's treasure, the mirror image of himself, sinks drowning into raw, liquid sin. Jehovah's stored rage against humankind from every century explodes in a single direction.

"Father! Father! Why have you forsaken me?!"

But heaven stops its ears. The Son stares up at the One who cannot, who will not, reach down or reply.

The Trinity had planned it. The Son endured it.

The Spirit enabled him. The Father rejected the Son whom he loved. Jesus, the God-man from Nazareth, perished. The Father accepted his sacrifice for sin and was satisfied. The Rescue was accomplished.

Don't move too quickly from this scene. Keep gazing.

The Rescue accomplished here was for *you*. John Stott writes, "Before we can begin to see the cross as something done *for* us (leading us to faith and worship), we have to see it as something done *by* us (leading us to repentance).... As we face the cross, then, we can say to ourselves both '*I* did it; my sins sent Him there,' and '*He* did it; His love took Him there.'"

Did you see your own offenses on the list of sins that necessitated the Cross? If not, name them yourself. Name your darkest sin. Now reflect on the fact that Christ bore the punishment for *that* sin. He took the punishment you deserved. Do you feel His passionate and specific love for *you*? He died for *you*. He was condemned and cursed so that you could go free—He was forsaken by God so that you would *never* be forsaken (Hebrews 13:5).

That's what Jesus' death on the cross has to do with our past sexual sin *right now*.

What Doesn't Work

Before we can embrace the grace and forgiveness shown us through Christ's atoning death, we have to forsake all the *wrong* ways of thinking and living that many of us have adopted—wrong ways that attempt to deal with sin apart from the Cross.

Let's look at the three wrong and ineffective ways man tries to deal with past sin and compare them with the strikingly different way that God revealed at Calvary.

1. Minimizing Sin

Man's way is to minimize sin. We try to escape our guilt by pretending that what we have done really isn't so bad. We change our morals to fit our behavior. We downplay sin and never call it what it really is. Instead, we say that we were "wild" when we were young. We blame our actions on our unseen and unaccountable "hormones." Sin isn't so serious, we assure ourselves. Besides, "we're only human."

But the Cross declares that *sin is serious.* God never downplays it. Sexual sin is the abuse of our bodies, which are made in His image—it is high treason against our almighty Maker. In fact, it's such a big deal that the only way for it to be justly dealt with is either for us sinners to spend an eternity in hell, or for the Son of God to receive the full wrath of God in our place. The Cross shows that our sin and guiltiness can't be minimized.

2. Ignoring Holiness

Another wrong way man excuses sin is to ignore God's holiness—to assume that God is as tolerant of sin as we are. This approach is most popular among "religious people," who would never *completely* reject God, but still don't want to be bothered by the idea of a righteous judge who is holy and calls them to be holy (1 Peter 1:15–16). Instead, we make God in our image and pretend that, like us, He's willing to overlook sin.

Again, the Cross contradicts man's approach. It shows that God's holiness can't be ignored. The torture and suffering inflicted on Jesus show just how much God hates our sin. God says, "These things you have done and I kept silent; you thought I was altogether like you. But I will rebuke you and accuse you to your face" (Psalm 50:21). God isn't like us. He's holy. And His standards haven't changed over time. He hasn't succumbed to popular opinion or decreased His holiness. He *remains* holy. The Cross reveals just how holy He is.

3. Living Self-Righteously

Man's third wrong approach to sin is self-righteousness. This can be expressed in several different ways. It's seen in the life of the person who is shocked that he was capable of sinning. "I just can't believe I did it," he says. Why is he so surprised? Because he self-righteously viewed himself as *basically good* instead of *inherently wicked.* Sadly, his grief over sin isn't because he has disobeyed God, but because he has failed to live up to his own inflated opinion of himself.

Self-righteousness is also expressed by the person who refuses to accept God's forgiveness. "I just can't forgive myself," she says. "Maybe God can, but I can't." It might appear pious, but statements like these are really a form of reverse pride that says, "My standards are higher than God's." Instead of humbly acknowledging that her sin was against God and that only He can wipe it away, she tries to become her own savior. She tries to bear her own punishment, pay penance by wallowing in guilt or doing good deeds, or add to God's favor through obedience.

But the Cross, as John Stott tells us, undermines our

self-righteousness. If we had any righteousness of our own, God wouldn't have needed to send a savior and substitute. God's plan of salvation very clearly reveals one thing: We have *nothing* to do with the Great Rescue. In fact, the only thing we contribute is the sin that has to be paid for. No man or woman can earn his or her salvation. No human born in sin is able to make amends. We can't pay enough penance; we can't do enough good works; we can't add to God's favor through our obedience.

The Cross humbles us. The only way God could give us right standing before Him was to transfer our guilt to Jesus and impute Jesus' perfect record to us.

Not only do minimizing sin, ignoring God's holiness, and living self-righteously not work, they can destroy your relationship. If you have past sexual sin to confess, minimizing it will also trivialize the preciousness of God's gift of pure sex in marriage. If sexual sin is no big deal, sexual purity is no big deal either. In the same way, ignoring God's holiness sets your marriage up for disaster. If God doesn't care about your past unfaithfulness, what motivation does either of you have to be faithful after you're married? Self-righteousness is also poisonous. A marriage that isn't built around the Cross will be devoid of the grace, mercy, and humility that come when both husband and wife recognize their need for a Savior.

Transformed

You might be thinking, "Is all this talk about the Cross and my sin supposed to be good news?" Yes, it is! When we see just how dire our situation really is, the Great Rescue becomes all the more incredible.

Rebecca Pippert tells a story that illustrates the transforming power of a proper understanding of the Cross:

Several years ago after I had finished speaking at a conference, a lovely woman came to the platform. She obviously wanted to speak to me and the moment I turned to her, tears welled up in her eyes. We made our way to a room where we could talk privately. It was clear from looking at her that she was sensitive but tortured. She sobbed as she told me the following story.

Years before, she and her fiancé (to whom she was now married) had been the youth workers at a large conservative church. They were a well-known couple and had an extraordinary impact on the young people. Everyone looked up to them and admired them tremendously. A few months before they were to be married they began having sexual relations. That left them burdened enough with a sense of guilt and hypocrisy. But then she discovered she was pregnant. "You can't imagine what the implications would have been of admitting this to our church," she said. "To confess that we were preaching one thing and living another would have been intolerable. The congregation was so conservative and had never been touched by any scandal. We felt they wouldn't be able to handle knowing about our situation. Nor could we bear the humiliation.

"So we made the most excruciating decision I have ever made. I had an abortion. My wedding day was the worst day of my entire life. Everyone in the church was smiling at me, thinking me a bride beaming in innocence. But do you know what was going through my head as I walked down the aisle? All I could think to myself was, 'You're a murderer. You were so proud that you couldn't bear the shame and humiliation of being exposed for what you are. But I know what you are and so does God. You have murdered an innocent baby.'"

She was sobbing so deeply that she could not speak. As I put my arms around her a thought came to me very strongly. But I was afraid to say it. I knew if it was not from God that it could be very destructive. So I prayed silently for the wisdom to help her.

She continued, "I just can't believe that I could do something so horrible. How could I have murdered an innocent life? How is it possible I could do such a thing? I love my husband; we have four beautiful children. I know the Bible says that God forgives all of our sins. But I can't forgive myself! I've confessed this sin a thousand times, and I still feel such shame and sorrow. The thought that haunts me the most is *how* could I murder an innocent life?"

I took a deep breath and said what I had been thinking. "I don't know why you are so surprised. This isn't the first time your sin has led to death; it's the second." She looked at me in utter amazement. "My dear friend," I continued, "when you look at the cross, all of us show up as crucifiers. Religious or nonreligious, good or bad, aborters or nonaborters—all of us are responsible for the death of the only innocent who ever lived. Jesus died for all of our sins—past, present, and future. Do you think there are any sins of yours that Jesus didn't have to die for? The very sin of pride that caused you to destroy your child is what killed Christ as well. It does not matter that you weren't there two thousand years ago. We all sent him there. Luther said that we carry his very nails in our pockets. So if you have done it before, then why couldn't you do it again?"

She stopped crying. She looked me straight in the eyes and said, "You're absolutely right. I have done something even worse than killing my baby. My sin is what drove Jesus to the cross. It doesn't matter that I wasn't there pounding in the nails, I'm still responsible for his death. Do you realize the significance of what you are telling me, Becky? I came to you saying I had done the worst thing imaginable. And you tell me I have done something even worse than that."

I grimaced because I knew this was true. (I am not sure that my approach would qualify as one of the great counseling techniques!) Then she said, "But Becky, if the cross shows me that I am far worse than I had ever imagined, it also shows me that my evil has been absorbed and forgiven. If the worst thing any human can do is to kill God's Son, and *that* can be forgiven, then how can anything else—even my abortion—not be forgiven?"

I will never forget the look in her eyes as she sat back in awe and quietly said, "Talk about amazing grace." This time she wept not out of sorrow but from relief and gratitude. I saw a woman literally transformed by a proper understanding of the cross.

Just like the woman in this story, we need to hear the bad news of the Cross before we can receive the good news. And for sinners like you and me, there's almost too much good news to take in.

Getting Practical

I want to show you three wonderful—and very practical— ways that a proper understanding of the Cross can affect your relationship.

1. Because of the Cross, you can be absolutely sure of God's love for you and His complete forgiveness of your past sin.

The Bible tells us the steps to take to receive God's grace. First, we must repent of our sin and ask Him to forgive us. Second, by faith we believe that Jesus died in our place and rose again.

If you've done this, guess what? You *are* forgiven. It's finished. First John 1:9 says, "If we confess our sins, he is faithful and just and will forgive us our sins and purify us from all unrighteousness." There's no probation time, no trial period. Yes, you may suffer from ongoing consequences in your life because of sin, but there will be no punishment from God. Christ has taken every last drop of God's wrath.

And your forgiveness is real whether you feel it or not. Recently I helped produce a three-part video series based on *I Kissed Dating Goodbye*. On the second tape, entitled "Purity," I asked my friend Travis to share the story of how he had experienced God's forgiveness for sexual sin. The story he humbly told was a compelling testimony of how the Cross overcomes feelings of condemnation.

"When I look at myself," Travis said, "there's no question that I'm overwhelmed at my own unworthiness. But when I remind myself of what God's Word says to me and what His promises are—that He is faithful when I have been faithless and that His kindness and mercy to me are based not on what I have done, but on the righteousness of His Son— that's when I realize that it's true whether I feel it or not. That's when I am saved from condemnation."

Travis has to *constantly* remind himself of the good news of God's grace. "I am often tempted," he confesses. "I look around at the friends I have, and now the wife that I have, and I think, 'Lord, I don't deserve this.' And He reminds me, 'It's not what you've done; it's what my Son has done for you.'"

That's the heart of the good news of the Bible. Speak that truth to yourself every day. Take comfort in the words of assurance that God has written to you in Scripture:

Therefore, there is now no condemnation for those who are in Christ Jesus. (Romans 8:1)

"Come now, let us reason together," says the LORD. "Though your sins are like scarlet, they shall be as white as snow; though they are red as crimson, they shall be like wool." (Isaiah 1:18)

He does not treat us as our sins deserve or repay us according to our iniquities. For as high as the heavens are above the earth, so great is his love for those who fear him; as far as the east is from the west, so far has he removed our transgressions from us. (Psalm 103:10–12)

In the light of the Cross, the Bible's promises take on a whole new brilliancy, don't they? You are pure and spotless before the Lord. Your sin has been removed from you an immeasurable distance—as far as the east is from the west.

My favorite promise is in Isaiah 43:25, where God says, "I, even I, am he who blots out your transgressions, for my own sake, and remembers your sins no more." Think about that! God *consciously* chooses not to remember your past. Jay Adams says that this means that God will *never* bring it up to you, *never* use it against you, and *never* reveal it to anyone else. When you come to Him in prayer, He doesn't label you as a fornicator or an adulterer—He doesn't see you as dirty and unworthy of His love. He sees you wearing the righteousness of His Son. Through faith in Christ's work at the cross, you can "approach God with freedom and confidence" (Ephesians 3:12). God now rejoices over you like a groom rejoices over his bride (Isaiah 62:5).

You are clean. You are totally forgiven. You are His. Your past has no claim on you because God has made you new. Never forget it. Never doubt it. Never stop rejoicing at the miracle of God's grace.

2. Because of the Cross you can confess your past sin to your partner.

No question about it—telling the man or woman you love about past sexual sin is difficult. It might mean confessing a lie you told earlier. It might cause him or her to reject you and end the relationship. How can the truth of the Cross help? The answer is that it puts things in perspective.

The biggest problem in your life is not whether a particular man or woman accepts you, but whether the God of the universe forgives you. The Cross shows that your biggest problem—God's wrath—has been taken care of. Confidence and security in God's love can give you the courage to confess your sin to someone else with the knowledge that *God* has forgiven you.

Telling me about her past was one of the hardest things Shannon had ever done. But she was able to do it because she knew that God, the person her sin had offended the most, had forgiven her. If I had rejected her, she would not have been devastated, because her ultimate security was found in the blood-bought acceptance of her Father in heaven.

When you reach the point where you know that God has forgiven you and you are ready to tell the person you love about your past, you still need to ask yourself some practical, if difficult, questions. First, *when* should you confess past sins? Next, *how much* should you disclose?

The decision of when you tell the person you're courting

about your past is based on several different factors. First, your primary motive should be to serve them. Your goal is to tell them early enough that they won't feel pressured because of promises they made before they got the information. For this reason, I think it's best to confess things of a serious nature *before* getting engaged. If you've already gotten engaged, you should come clean as soon as possible.

This doesn't mean that you're obligated to share intimate details of your life as soon as your courtship begins. Obviously, you should do so only if the relationship is clearly headed toward marriage. If you've reached the point where you are confident that you would like the relationship to lead to marriage, it's probably time to talk about past sin.

The next question is how much detail you should give in your confession. The authors of *Preparing for Marriage* have several helpful pieces of advice:

- First, write a list of what you need to confess. "This might include events, choices, or hurts you've experienced. While you don't need to go into great detail, be sure to mention anything that you know will affect your relationship today."

- Decide which items on your list you should share with the person you're courting (or engaged to) and why. Shannon sought the advice of Julie, a godly married lady from church, about what she should tell me. Julie's support and counsel were very important to Shannon.

- Set a time and place to talk that will be private. You want a setting where you are both free to express your emotions. Before the meeting, ask God to give the one you love the grace to respond in love. Don't expect this to be easy for them. Appeal for their forgiveness, but don't demand it. Give them time.

- Don't tell more than will serve the other person. "As you talk," the authors of *Preparing for Marriage* write, "explain why you think it's important to share these choices from your past, but avoid sharing more than is necessary. Be careful about sharing too many explicit details, as this can become a problem later in your marriage. By going into too much detail, you may give the one you love too much of the picture. Avoid morbid curiosity." This is something Shannon did very well. She told me all that I needed to know but encouraged me not to probe for information that would only torture my imagination later.

- Finally, be patient with the ones to whom you confess your sin. Give them time to appropriate God's grace and examine their heart's response to your confession. Chances are they will struggle. They might pull away from you for a period of time. In some cases, they may even end the relationship. If that happens, try to remember that it's better that you worked through this now than after marriage. Use it as an opportunity to remind yourself how differently God has responded to your sin. He has embraced you and promised never to leave you. His love is unfailing. And at the right time, He can bring a man or woman into your life who will accept you and forgive your past.

3. Because of the Cross, you can forgive the past sin of another person.

If you are the person receiving the confession in your relation-ship, I understand what a challenge this can be—especially if you have saved yourself sexually. I certainly wouldn't have been a virgin if I hadn't grown up a Christian, and I had sus-pected that Shannon wasn't a virgin when we first began our courtship. Still, I experienced a very deep sense of sorrow when she told me about her past relationships. I loved her. Sin had stolen something from us that couldn't be replaced. That was very sad for both of us.

If you're having to work through another person's past sin, let me encourage you to consider several things.

First, you have the opportunity to be a channel of God's forgiveness. Though it's easy to see only how their sin affects you, remember that it's probably twice as hard for him or her to tell you as it is for you to listen. Keep reminding them of the reality of God's forgiveness. As you process your own feelings, continually point them to the Cross and make sure they're rooted in an understanding of God's grace.

Second, don't allow what can be an appropriate sense of loss and disappointment at the effects of sin turn into self-righteousness or bitterness toward the other person. You may be a virgin, but you too are a sinner who can only be saved by the atoning death of Jesus.

Though the sin of the one you love does affect you if you choose to get married, keep in mind that the sin was primarily against God. He was there to witness it. He wept over it. At the cross, He bled over it. He loves your partner more than you ever can. And He has forgiven him or her. Don't hold yourself above God by withholding your forgiveness.

Third, while you should forgive the man or woman you're in a relationship with, you shouldn't equate forgiveness with an obligation to get married. Depending on where you are in your relationship, there might still be questions to answer before getting engaged. Don't let this issue cause you to overlook other areas of concern.

I know of cases where the man or woman just couldn't deal with the fact that the other person had slept with other people. If you're not able to forgive and move beyond this issue, don't assume that getting married will fix the problem. Take your time; get counsel. If you can't reconcile it, be willing to end the relationship.

Finally, if you do choose to get married, make sure that you forgive like God does—choose to remember their past sin no more. As humans, we can't do it perfectly like God does, but we can refuse to dwell on the past. When it comes to mind, we can push it away. As Jay Adams says, "Forgiveness is a promise, not a feeling."

When you forgive other people, you're making a promise not to use their past sin against them. My dad's advice to me before Shannon and I were engaged was very helpful. "You need to settle in your heart," he said, "that you will *never*—whether it's in the heat of an argument or under any circumstances—use her past as a weapon." That's the commitment I made, and by God's grace I've kept it.

Mourn with Those Who Mourn

When Shannon told me about her life before becoming a Christian, I never wavered in my desire to continue our relationship. I loved her. I knew that God had saved her and changed her, and I believed that He was leading us to become husband and wife.

But just because I had forgiven her and was confident about our future didn't mean that I didn't struggle at times with her past. In fact, some of the hardest days for me came after we were engaged. As the time grew nearer for Shannon to become my bride, the reality of what was lost touched me in a new way. I began to fear that Shannon would compare me to her past boyfriends. I was hurting and needed reassurance.

I share this with you to say that after you're done confessing and forgiving each other, you're still going to need each other. You'll both face unique temptations. In our relationship, Shannon continued to deal with condemnation. She needed me to remind her that I had forgiven her and that God had cleansed her. At the same time, I needed to hear her tell me that she loved me and that her past relationships were meaningless to her.

But the most important thing we learned was that ultimately the comfort we each longed for could come only from God. We did need each other, and we did extend grace and support to each other. But only God Himself could bring true peace and final closure to the past. I couldn't be Shannon's ultimate source of assurance. And Shannon couldn't be mine. She couldn't say "I love you" or "The other guys don't matter" enough times to bring my heart peace. I had to look to God and find that peace in Him.

Two Sinners at the Foot of the Cross

Some of the best and most realistic advice I received was from a friend who had gone through a similar experience with his wife. He simply said, "The sting lessens. You'll always have a sense of regret, but over time the pain decreases till it's hardly there."

He was right. Before Shannon and I were married, there were days when, tortured by my own imagination of Shannon's past relationships, I could only lie on my bed and cry to God for mercy. The sting was sharp and painful. But it has lessened. In fact, it has nearly disappeared. Today I rarely, if ever, even think about it. When I do, there's sadness, but greater than the sadness is my joy at how God has rescued both Shannon and me.

For us the memory of our difficult conversation and the days that followed is bittersweet. Bitter because sin really does destroy and ruin life; sweet because in the moment of our deepest shared grief, the mercy and grace of God was never more real to us. The pain of the past caused us both to draw closer to the cross of our Savior Jesus. The gospel became more real, more cherished, more powerful than ever before.

Is it possible to outrun the past? No. But when you know the forgiveness and grace of God, it is possible to face it without fear. For Shannon and me, the past still comes knocking. But when it does, we don't open the door on our own. We look to our crucified and risen Savior, and we ask Him to answer it for us.

We started our marriage, and hope to always remain, in awe of grace—two sinners at the foot of the cross.

Chapter Eleven

ARE YOU READY FOR FOREVER?

Ten Questions to Answer Before You Get Engaged

S tack up all the choices you'll ever make in life—which school you attend, which job you take, which friends you choose, which car or house you buy—and they're dwarfed by the decision about which person you marry. Your marriage will join you body and soul to another human. Your marriage will determine the mother or father of your future children. It can strengthen or hinder your effectiveness for God. It can bring you a lifetime of joy or leave you miserable.

That's why we have to keep reminding ourselves of the real questions we're facing. The questions are not: "Do we want to have sex?" or "Would we enjoy the excitement of getting engaged and planning a wedding?" or "Do all our friends and family expect us to get married?"

The *real* questions are: "Are we ready to care for, sacrifice for, and love each other through good times and bad?" and "Do we believe that we would glorify God more as a couple than as individuals?" and "Are we ready for forever?"

Many people are unhappily married because they failed to ask the important questions. Instead of soberly evaluating their relationship, they got caught up in the excitement of the moment. They ignored reality when they were dating, only to spend their marriage complaining about it. As Alexander Pope wrote, "They dream in courtship and in wedlock wake."

The season of courtship is the time to be wide awake, with your eyes wide open. This doesn't mean being hyper-critical or judgmental. Instead, it means soberly and honestly evaluating ourselves, the other person, and our relationship before we commit ourselves to marriage.

Questions to Ask Before You Buy the Ring

The ten questions that follow can wake you up to the current condition of your relationship. Many of them are taken from what we've discussed in previous chapters. I've also borrowed heavily from an article entitled "Should We Get Married?" by David Powlison, a skilled Christian counselor, and John Yenchko, his pastor. (This article is also available from Resources for Changing Lives as a booklet entitled *Pre-Engagement: 5 Questions to Ask Yourselves.*) These two men, who possess much more wisdom and experience than I, have very generously given me permission to quote them extensively.

I encourage you to approach these questions humbly and with a desire to grow. Working through these ten questions as a couple, as well as individually, can help you discover both strengths and weaknesses in your relationship and help you make a more informed decision about whether you should get married.

1. Is your relationship centered on God and His glory?

Is Jesus Christ the Lord of both your hearts? A happy marriage is founded on mutual love for and submission to Him. Are you obedient to His Word? Are both of you striving to find your soul's satisfaction in God? If you aren't, you'll enter marriage with the false expectation that it will fulfill and complete you. You'll put unrealistic demands on your spouse by asking him or her to play a role only Christ can fill.

2. Are you growing in friendship, communication, fellowship, and romance?

Score your relationship in the four areas we looked at in chapters 5 and 6:

Friendship. Do you enjoy being together? Apart from your romantic feelings, do you have a solid foundation of friendship? Are there activities and interests that draw you together? If you were the same sex, do you think you'd be friends?

Communication. Have you grown in your ability to hear and understand each other? Every relationship will have room for improvement; the question is, do you see growth?

Fellowship. Do you talk about spiritual things? Do you

pray together? Do you love God more today as a result of your relationship?

Romance. Are you growing in your romantic desire for each other? Are your affections increasing? If they aren't, why do you think they're absent? Are you trying to make the relationship work when your heart really isn't in it?

3. Are you clear on your biblical roles as man and woman?

Do both of you have a biblical conviction about what it means to be a godly man or godly woman? Are you in agreement about the role of husband and wife? When you read chapter 7, were their any parts you reacted to or disagreed with? Talk about them together.

If you're a woman, ask yourself if this man is someone you could respect, submit to, and love. The Bible assigns a wife two primary responsibilities: to respect and submit to her husband (Ephesians 5:22–24; Colossians 3:18). These two responsibilities are closely linked. If you respect your husband, submitting to him will be a joy. If you don't respect him, submission will be burdensome.

If you're a man, are you currently initiating and leading in the relationship? Do you have the faith to lead this woman and serve her in love for a lifetime? You need to make sure that she can and will follow your spiritual leadership.

4. Are other people supportive of your relationship?

Have you had the protection and support of your local church in your courtship? Please don't move forward with engagement before getting counsel from people who know you well.

Powlison and Yenchko write:

> Good counsel helps you carefully and prayerfully think through the decision. It sorts out whether your main reasons for marrying are self-centered, or if you know how to commit yourself to love someone else. Good counsel helps you identify potential problem areas and work on them now.

5. Is sexual desire playing too big (or too small) a part in your decision?

Sexual involvement before marriage can muddle clear thinking. Someone has said, "Never let a fool kiss you or a kiss fool you." Has sexual desire fooled you into believing that your relationship is better than it really is? Or is looking forward to sex a primary motive in wanting to get married? Sex is obviously a very important part of marriage, but remember that it can't make up for weaknesses in other parts of a relationship.

While sexual desire shouldn't play too big a part, it shouldn't be too small, either. It's important that you are sexually attracted to your spouse. As my dad likes to say, we shouldn't try to be "more spiritual than God" and marry someone we aren't excited about going to bed with.

6. Do you have a track record of solving problems biblically?

David Powlison and John Yenchko ask:

Do you act like godly adults, or like self-centered children when facing disagreements, misunderstandings, or decisions? Failure to solve problems biblically shows up in lots of obvious ways. Do you manipulate? Do you avoid facing problems? Do you whitewash matters by pretending everything is okay? Do you store up resentments?

If you see wrong patterns in your relationship, it doesn't necessarily mean that you should end it, but you do need to be cautious and seek to change. Good marriages are not devoid of conflict. What is important is that both people are committed to resolving problems according to God's Word.

What does it mean to solve problems biblically? It starts with a basic understanding of what the Bible teaches about the major areas of life. It means knowing how to bring up and talk through difficult issues. It means being willing to ask forgiveness for your contribution to the problem, no matter what the other person has done.

Don't move ahead unless you see progress in this part of your relationship.

7. Are you heading in the same direction in life?

"When the Bible speaks of marriage," write Powlison and Yenchko, "it speaks four times of 'leaving and cleaving.' *Leaving* means you are no longer tied to the direction set by your parents and your single life. *Cleaving* means you choose to move in the same direction as your spouse."

Powlison and Yenchko point out that they're not making an argument for the secular notion of "compatibility," which says that a relationship can only work if a man and woman come hatched out of the same mold.

Two very different people can have a wonderful marriage. But there are *basic* kinds of agreement that a man and woman come to in order to cleave to one another. Jesus says that we must count the cost of our decisions (Luke 14:28–29). Amos says, "Do two walk together unless they have agreed to do so?" (Amos 3:3).

Have you talked about what "leaving and cleaving" will mean if you get married? Courtship is the time to discuss how you would relate to your parents and your single friends as a married couple. Are you ready to let go of much of the individual freedom you've had as a single? How do you envision your shared life? Are you in agreement about lifestyle issues like religious beliefs and practice, children, church involvement, and money?

8. Have you taken into account any cultural differences you have?

Derrick and Lindsey had to work through the differences of a Korean and a Chinese upbringing. My friends Cori and Kathy got engaged only after they had seriously considered the challenges they would face in an interracial marriage—Cori is black, Kathy is white. Walking with Kathy on the street, Cori had been called a "sellout" by other blacks; Kathy had to patiently talk through the issue with her parents, who were initially opposed to the relationship. They're in love and have faith for marriage, but they had to stare the issue of their racial and cultural backgrounds in the face.

Are interracial marriages unbiblical? Definitely not. But

it's still important to carefully think through the implications for your future together.

9. Do either of you have complicating entanglements from past marriages or relationships?

We live in a time when many people bring the consequences of past relationships into the present. Are you committed to dealing with these issues on God's terms? David Powlison and John Yenchko write:

> There are "legal" divorces which Jesus views as illegitimate (Matthew 19:1–9). There are times when the Lord commands us to continue to pursue reconciliation rather than remarry (1 Corinthians 7:10–11). There are also situations in which God views the marriage as broken, and a person is free to consider remarrying (Matthew 5:31–32; 1 Corinthians 7:12–16, 39; Romans 7:2–3).
>
> All the ins and outs of these questions go beyond the scope of our discussion here. But if you have prior entanglements (for example, a prior marriage or children out of wedlock), you must think through the implications of what the Lord says. Seek pastoral counsel from others who will take the biblical passages seriously. Ideally the church should make a declaration that a person is or is not free to remarry.

10. Do you want to marry this person?

"The Bible tells us that the decision to marry is a choice we make," write Powlison and Yenchko. "The final questions you should ask yourself are, 'Do I *want* to marry this person?' and 'Does this person *want* to marry me?'"

Why do two skilled counselors ask what seems like such a basic question? Because they've seen too many couples overspiritualize the decision of whom they marry. Instead of realizing that God leads us by providing wisdom and allowing us to make our own choices, these couples wait for a "mystical experience" that will tell them what to do. Countering this mindset Powlison and Yenchko write:

> Getting married is *your* choice. You are the one who will affirm vows and say "I do." No one—and no "leading"—can constrain or compel you to make these vows.
>
> First Corinthians 7:25–40 is the lengthiest passage in the Bible that explicitly speaks of how people decide to get married. It is filled with phrases such as: "He should do as he wants, he is not sinning"; "The man who has settled the matter in his own mind, who is under no compulsion but who has control over his own will, and who has made up his mind"; "She is free to marry anyone she wishes, but he must belong to the Lord."

Could it be any clearer? God expects you to make the decision. And God promises to bless you and work out His will in your life through your decisions.

Finally, David Powlison and John Yenchko remind couples that their yes is to a person, not to a "fantasy woman" or to "the man I hope he will become." They write:

Ask yourself, "Am I willing to accept this person as he or she is? Do I want to marry *this* person?" Make sure that you are not coming to marriage with a hidden agenda, expecting to change the other person once you are married. Are you saying yes to a real person, with weaknesses as well as strengths, sins as well as gifts?

Wanting the Best

When two people are in love, questions like the ones we've just looked at can seem tiresome. But while they might seem to rain on the parade of romantic ardor, they really are important. What I hope you realize is that carefully thinking through these and other issues is an expression of Christlike love for each other. There's nothing loving about walking into marriage with your eyes closed. Examination will strengthen a healthy relationship.

Do you really want what's best for each other? Then you'll welcome the chance to honestly evaluate it, even if it means you discover some potential problems.

When the Answer Is No

After reading this chapter, maybe you've realized that you don't want to marry the person you're in a courtship with. Miguel and Elena had courted three months when they decided to call off their relationship. "We appreciated each other as friends," Miguel explains. "But when we spent more time together one-on-one, we discovered that we were very different and just didn't complement each other. Our courtship helped us see that we weren't meant to go further than friendship."

I know this can be very difficult, but if you're having doubts about your relationship, please don't be afraid to admit it. Remember, you're under no obligation to get married. A successful courtship is one in which two people treat each other with holiness and sincerity and make a wise choice about marriage—whether the choice is yes or no.

What should you do if you think you're supposed to end a relationship? Besides continuing to pray, I encourage you to discuss your reservations with a trusted Christian friend who can help you process your feelings. Don't ask him or her to try to convince you one way or the other. You just need someone who can listen to your concerns and help you identify why you're lacking faith for marriage.

Next, if you realize you don't want to get married (even if engagement hasn't been brought up), the courtship should end. Every day that a courtship continues is an unspoken statement that both people are growing in their confidence for marriage. If either person loses this confidence, he or she owes it to the other person to halt the courtship.

When you end the courtship, communicate your thoughts and feelings with the motive of serving the other person. Ask for God's help to choose the right words. Consider writing out your thoughts beforehand so you can make sure to communicate clearly. If there are any ways in which you feel you have misled or hurt the other person, humbly confess it and ask for forgiveness.

It's also important that you be clear about the status of

the relationship. If the courtship is over, make sure the other person understands that you're not just putting it on pause. My friend John was vague when he ended his courtship. For more than a year the girl held out hope that the relationship would pick back up. John realized that he selfishly liked the idea of having her as a "backup," should he change his mind. He apologized and made it clear that they would only be friends in the future.

Life-Rocking, but Not Life-Ending

But what if you're the person being broken up with? What if you would like the relationship to continue, but the other person wants to end it? How do you handle that? "It can be a real life-rocker," thirty-four-year-old Pam admits. "People need to realize that their hearts will recover. They can get over it. God is sovereign. It is not the end of life."

When Gary ended their relationship, my friend Evelyn struggled with self-pity and disappointment. But she realized that the fact that she felt devastated showed that she'd been hoping for too much from the relationship. God helped her find comfort in His unchanging character and love.

And though it was difficult at first, she and Gary have been able to relate again as friends. "My biggest prayer after we broke up was, 'Lord, I don't want to grow bitter toward him,'" Evelyn told me afterwards. "It's hard. But today we're good friends. That's possible because of the way Gary led during our courtship. Our hearts weren't engaged prematurely."

The same is true of Miguel and Elena. Today both look back on their courtship without regret. "Miguel treated me as a sister the whole time," Elena remembers. "Breaking up was hard at the time," she says. "You're hoping it will work, so it's disappointing when it doesn't. But in the midst of the disappointment there was joy. We knew God had someone else for each of us. I remember Miguel saying, 'I will be cheering when God brings you your husband.' I knew he really meant it."

The Courage to Obey

Has your confidence for marriage increased or decreased as a result of reading this chapter? Whatever your circumstances, I hope that your commitment to act on what you have seen has become stronger.

It requires faith and courage to end a relationship just as it does to pursue a courtship. In a chapter entitled "The Courage to Stay Single," Eva McAllaster shares stories of single men and women who made the difficult choice to end relationships that weren't right.

McAllaster writes:

Mara had the courage. She was already wearing a diamond when she began to realize that Larry's moods were so unpredictable that, in spite of all the qualities for which she adored him, he was not good husband material. Nor was he ready to be a father. She thought of his moods—those black moods—and she shuddered, and she stood by her courage.

I pray that you'll have this kind of courage and that you'll be willing to stand by what God has shown you about the relationship you're in. Don't let pressure from others, fear of being alone, or a craving for marriage lead you to make a foolish decision. Trust God's guidance and be courageous.

That courage could also involve taking the plunge into marriage. An adventure of faith lies ahead of that course too. Maybe God has been confirming the goodness of your relationship, but you're afraid of the unknown. Or maybe your parents were divorced, and you think it's inevitable that your marriage will fail as well. That simply is not true. By God's grace, you can overcome your past and your own sinful tendencies and build a successful marriage.

If you've honestly answered the important questions and God's Spirit is giving you peace about pursuing marriage, don't let fear hold you back.

Ask her!

If he proposes, say yes!

Live courageously!

When you know in your heart that you've found the person you want to spend the rest of your life with, forever can't start soon enough.

———

Chapter Twelve

THAT DAY

Living and Loving in Light of Eternity

My face is sore from smiling. My heart is beating as though I just ran a hundred-yard dash. But I'm standing still. Trying to stand tall. Waiting.

And then, the music soars. A door at the back of the church auditorium opens. I catch a glimpse of white, and I quiver.

This is the moment.

Every head turns. Necks crane. The congregation rises in unison.

There is Shannon, leaning on her father's arm. She seems to glow.

If only there were a pause button I could press to make this scene stand still. Only for a moment, just long enough to try to take it in. I want to savor every second.

Today is my wedding day. My bride has just walked into view.

My *bride*. My bride.

So *this* is the dress I've waited to see. It's gorgeous. If I were a girl, I'd be able to describe it. I'd know enough to say that it's satin with an empire waist and chiffon overlay that opens down the front. I'd rave about delicate lace around the neck and shoulders and its chapel-length train. But I'm just a boy. And all I know to say is that the dress is incredible. She makes it stunning.

Beneath her veil I see a smile. It's for me. She is for me.

My mind is straining to record this scene. How quickly it will become a memory. *Don't miss a detail. This is the moment.*

Oh, Lord, she's beautiful.

The Beginning

A wedding—a beginning. Nearly two years have passed since our beginning. Two years since Shannon walked down the aisle. Two years since we bound our hearts and lives in solemn vows before God.

"You think you're in love now," older couples told us then. "Just wait…it gets even better." They were right. It does get better. And we've only just begun. We have so much ahead of us. So much to learn. Some days we feel like a pair of kindergartners. Young at love. Inexperienced. Each day discovering just how little we know, but happy because we're learning together.

The one thing we know for certain is that marriage is a very good thing. God's plan for two to become one was pure genius. Even as a newlywed, I've seen its rightness in a thousand different moments. When Shannon's foot slides to my side of the bed in the middle of the night and rests against me. When she laughs with me at an inside joke about another inside joke, the origin of which neither of us can remember. When she puts her finger on an anxiousness in my heart that no one else, not even me, has seen. When I come home at the end of the day and know she's waiting for me.

Yes, marriage can be very good.

A wonderful, God-blessed, God-honoring marriage is what it's all about. And it's the potential for just that that makes it worth the effort to do the courtship right. A godly courtship establishes habits and patterns that can continue on until "death do us part." This is why we want to make God's glory our priority. This is why we want to grow in friendship. This is why we want to love righteousness and flee temptation. Because these are the qualities we want to define our marriages.

The romantic pursuit doesn't end with the marriage ceremony. Till my dying day, I want to be working to win Shannon's heart, to grow closer to her as a friend, to be more skilled as a lover. We've only just begun.

When Will My Turn Come?

You've come to the end of this book. You've read the stories of many different couples. What about you? Where are you in your story?

Maybe you feel like you're waiting for it to begin. Maybe reading all the happy endings has been a painful reminder that you're still alone.

"Boy meets girl" hasn't happened to you. You haven't met the right woman. The right man hasn't come along. Or if he did, he failed to notice you. *I'm glad you're enjoying marriage, Josh,* you might be thinking, *but what about me?*

I won't pretend to know all the disappointments you've faced. I don't know what you've been through or how long you've waited. Every day I get letters from men and women who have waited far longer than I did and experienced much more pain. I don't have easy answers. "All I ever wanted was to be married," a woman wrote me. "I thought it would have happened by now." The honesty with which she confessed her struggle was heartbreaking:

I used to wonder, "What's wrong with me?" but now I'm wondering what's right. I asked God to take away my burning desire for marriage if it's not His plan for me, but He hasn't.

I've never admitted this because I feel so ashamed, but I've stopped going to weddings, because jealousy gets the best of me. The last wedding I attended just overwhelmed me. All went well until the end when the pastor said, "You may kiss your bride for the first time." The groom lifted her veil, and everyone was expecting them to just go ahead and kiss, but they didn't. Instead he slowly cupped her face in his hands, and they just stood there looking deep into each other's eyes. I could almost hear their secret communication. Then they smiled and kissed, long and deeply.

At that point, I lost it. The tears poured from my eyes, and I sobbed in silence. The lump in my throat was so huge that I could only manage to squeak out a few words to the bride in the reception line. No one suspected that I was so jealous; they thought I was being sentimental. But she knew. While tears ran down my face, she looked at me sympathetically and then put her arms around me and held me tight.

I left the reception early. When I got home I fell across my bed and cried. "When will it be my turn, Lord?"

Are you asking that question? "When will it be *my* turn? When will *my* story begin?"

If you're single, I believe that God wants you to see that your story *has* begun. Life doesn't start when you find a spouse. Marriage is wonderful, but it's simply a new chapter in life. It's just a new way to do what we're all created to do— to live for and glorify our Creator.

Right now God is working all the elements of your life together for your good (Romans 8:28). This time in your life is part of your story. Maybe it's not what you had planned. Maybe you wish your Prince or Princess would have arrived by now. But God is right on schedule. He knows exactly what He's doing. He sees you right where you are. He hasn't forgotten you. He hasn't overlooked you. The circumstances you're going through—no matter how difficult—are part of the very happy ending He has planned.

God is greater than your circumstances. My pastor, C. J. Mahaney, once told a group of singles: "Your greatest need is not a spouse. Your greatest need is to be delivered from the wrath of God—and that has already been accomplished for you through the death and resurrection of Christ. So why doubt that God will provide a much, much lesser need? Trust His sovereignty, trust His wisdom, trust His love."

I don't have any pat answers. I can only urge you to trust Him.

Trust God's *sovereignty*. He sees your end from your beginning. His plan for your life can't be thwarted. He is in control.

Trust God's *wisdom*. If marriage is His will for you, He knows exactly what you need in a spouse. And in His unfathomable wisdom, He knows *when* you'll be ready. His timing will be perfect.

Trust God's *love*. Hasn't He given His very life to save you from sin? Hasn't He demonstrated His love on the cross? Then He can provide for your lesser needs too. Even your present trials are part of His loving plan for you. And whatever God has in store for tomorrow will be another perfect expression of His love.

Look into His Face

I'm inspired by my friend Kimberly. She's serving as a missionary to India with her parents. She wants to be married. She can't wait to be a mother. Though she loves the people of India and the work God has called her to, she often wrestles with doubt. Is India keeping her from finding a husband? Can God provide?

Recently she e-mailed me about a dream God gave her. It gave her renewed faith to trust Him. I hope it encourages you as well.

I saw the Creator's hands forming little me. The same hands that had created the stars and the heavens were carefully fashioning me. I was filled with wonder and gratefulness.

I wept as I continued to see myself, now a young lady, sitting in the center of His hand, knees drawn up to my chest, my head lifted to the Lover of my soul—my all in all. I was focused on Him and only Him. My gaze was filled by His face. And He looked as delighted as I was to have my *total* attention. I sat for what seemed an eternity, marveling and communing with my Savior, my eyes reveling in Him.

As I sat there, I saw, out of the corner of my eye, His other hand coming into view and in that hand I saw *him*. I knew who it was the instant I saw that it was a man. Simultaneously, we jumped to our feet and looked up at the Master.

"Is that him?" I asked. "The one I have been waiting for? The one who has been waiting for me? Is it him?"

I could hear that he was asking the same question about me. "Is that her? The one I have been waiting for? The one who has been waiting for me?"

Both of our voices quaked with excitement, but they could not compare to the joy and pleasure that was in God's voice as He smiled and said, "Yes." Bringing His hands close, He joined our hands and released us into the world…together.

"I can't tell you the joy and the peace the dream brought to my heart," Kimberly told me. For her, it was an affirmation and reminder of what the Bible clearly taught. God had shaped and formed her (Psalm 119:73). God knew her intimately (Psalm 139:2). Before anything else, God wanted her to look to Him for her soul's satisfaction (Psalm 42:1).

Kimberly told a few friends about her dream. Each one asked, "What did he look like? What did your husband look like?"

"I don't know," she answered them. "His face was never clear. But that's all right, because I know the face of the One that I am looking into right now and that is all that matters."

On That Day

Yes, that is all that matters. And even after marriage, it will continue to be the thing that matters most. When marriage is motivated by a passion to please God, it doesn't distract us. A godly marriage is a man and a woman, side by side in the hand of God's providence, gazing up to Him.

And then one day in heaven, when this life is done, you'll truly be able to see His face. You'll be able to look into His eyes. Imagine that conversation with Jesus. Do you think that on that day you'll question His plan for your life? Do you think you'll have grounds to accuse Him of stinginess or unfaithfulness? Do you think you'll complain that you had to wait so long for a spouse? Or even that you never married?

You won't do any of these things, because in heaven, you'll see and know the perfection of His plan for you. It won't be theoretical. It won't simply be a promise in the Bible. You'll see it as the undeniable fact that it is. What you'll tell Him on that day is that He was faithful. You'll say that His choices were exactly what you would have chosen knowing what you know now.

The Bible tells us that human history will culminate in a wedding (Revelation 19:7). We, the church, will be Christ's bride. At that celebration there will be no regret. No tears of sorrow. No man or woman will watch from afar wondering when his or her time will come. That moment will be *our* time—the time for which we were made. We will each treasure the unique story of grace that God wrote with our lives. And we'll see that *this* is the wedding all other weddings have hinted at. That *this* Groom is the One our hearts have always longed for.

Do you believe in *that* day? Then trust God *today*.

Ask yourself this: What would it look like for you to live in light of *that* day? What would it mean to live with a radical faith in God's goodness? What would you do differently than you are right now?

Would you stop worrying?

Would you stop complaining?

If you're a man, would you call her?

If you're a woman, would you wait for him to call? Would you let wisdom guide your romance?

Would you stop believing the lies of lust?

Would you end a relationship you know is wrong? Would you live courageously?

Would you say yes?

Picture your life lived in light of that day. Your story has already begun, but today could be a turning point. Today could be the day you choose to believe and obey God's Word with all your heart.

Our Story Is His Story

Shannon and I love to retell our love story. Not because we're the most dashing or impressive characters. Not because it's the most romantic story we've ever heard. We love it because it's our story of God's grace.

It's a story of how He saved us both from sin, and then brought us together from opposite sides of the country. How He heard our prayers and answered them. How He saw clearly when the future was obscure to us. How He knew with certainty when we were uncertain. How He was working when we were at a standstill.

We love to marvel at God's sovereignty. God saw me sitting in church listening to Shannon share the story of how she became a Christian. I couldn't have imagined it, but He knew that two years later we'd be getting married in the same auditorium.

God saw Shannon in the difficult months leading up to our courtship when, struggling with feelings for me, she would walk out of the church lobby with a heavy heart. He saw the tears she cried as she drove home. She couldn't have known, but God knew that only twelve months later she'd be walking out the same church doors as my wife—this time amidst a shower of white rose petals and to a car waiting to take us on our honeymoon.

We didn't know, but He knew. He knew all along.

On our wedding invitations we quoted a passage from Mike Mason's book *The Mystery of Marriage:*

Real love is always fated. It has been arranged before time. It is the most meticulously prepared of coincidences. And fate, of course, is simply a secular term for the will of God, and coincidence for His grace.

This is what we learned through our courtship. Our love story, like all real love stories, was arranged by God. All the coincidences that made it possible were interventions of His grace. Our story was His story.

In heaven, I won't be surprised if love stories are recounted. But the tales of "boy meets girl" won't be testimonies to the power of human love or goodness. Instead, they'll be testimonies to God's mercy, love, and kindness.

Straight Paths

My goal in this book hasn't been to unveil some method or program for relationships. I don't want reading it to make you passionate about courtship. What I hope is that you'll be more passionate about God—that you'll be more confident in His character and more excited about living for His glory.

I'm no expert. If you're single, I'm only a few steps ahead of you on this path. But I'm calling back to you with this encouragement: God's way really is best. His timing is perfect. Waiting on Him is more than worth it. Honoring Him and practicing His principles as you walk the path to marriage will lead you to the greatest joy and fulfillment.

I don't know the specific challenges you're facing or the pain you feel from past mistakes. Chances are your story will unfold very differently from mine. But Proverbs 3:5–6 gives a promise that is for all of us:

> Trust in the LORD with all your heart and lean not on
> your own understanding; in all your ways acknowl-
> edge him, and he will make your paths straight.

This promise was true in my life. It was true for Shannon.
Even though our trust wasn't perfect, God showed us that He
is completely worthy of our trust.

With This Ring

After we said our vows and exchanged rings as tokens of our
commitment, there was only one more thing to do. It had
seemed such a long time coming, but I finally heard our
pastor speak the words.

"Joshua and Shannon," he said, his own happiness evi-
dent in his voice, "having made a covenant before God and
with each other, I, in this moment acting with the authority
that has been invested in me by the Lord Jesus Christ and the
state of Maryland, pronounce you husband and wife."

Then he paused and smiled.

"Joshua, you have waited so many months for this
moment.

It is my joy to invite you now to please kiss your bride."

And so I did. And the wait didn't seem so long now that
she was in my arms.

It's a simple story, really.

Two people learning to trust God.

Two winding paths that God made straight.

Two straight paths that He chose to cross at just the
right time. We watched Him do that. For all the moments

of difficulty it involved, we wouldn't trade the experience for anything.

God wants to do the same for you.

Yes, you.

The Creator of romance, the Maker who arranged the first "boy meets girl" in the Garden so very long ago, is still at work.

COURTSHIP
CONVERSATIONS:
EIGHT GREAT DATES

with Heather and David Kopp

Pursuing romance with purpose takes planning and creativity. Sometimes we all feel like we're lacking both. Shannon and I remember the early days of our courtship. We were always looking for things we could do together that would be fun and help us get to know each other better. I wish I could say I always had a great plan, but too often I found myself racking my brain for an original question to ask and an interesting activity to share. I didn't find much help at the Christian bookstore. Most books with "date suggestions" either seemed juvenile or were for married couples and too steamy for a couple in the "hands-off" season of courtship.

These eight Courtship Conversations are what we wish we'd had back then. We think you'll find them a God-sent gift to your relationship. Our friends Heather and David Kopp did a terrific job planning not only things for you to do, but also great questions that will help you get to know each other, grow closer, and enjoy yourselves.

Using the Courtship Conversations is really simple: Use what seems helpful, ditch what doesn't. Here are a few more suggestions:

Talking. All of the areas covered in the conversations are important, but your relationship may process them in different ways. Go at the pace that's right for the two of you. If a conversation we suggest has already happened, or if a date or question seems too serious for where your relationship is, skip to something that works for you. All the questions are just suggestions—you probably won't talk through them all, or need to. Ask God to use this guide to spark the conversation you both need most.

Leading. Gentlemen, we suggest you serve by taking the lead in making these times happen. That doesn't mean you need to apply the date ideas or questions rigidly. Rather, be the gracious host who's making sure that your times and talks together are progressing well and that you're both having fun.

Listening. Of course, conversation isn't really happening unless there's as much careful listening as talking. So remember to listen well—not just with your ears, but prayerfully and genuinely, with your whole being.

Enjoying. If you've invited God to lead the way in your courtship, you can relax. For example, don't let yourselves feel like a failure if you don't/can't answer all the questions. God is at work! He is present with you, ready to lead you both toward your futures in quietness, confidence, and joy.

We hope you have a great time!

—*Josh and Shannon*

Courtship Conversation

#1

THE STORY OF ME

The Date: Each person gets one evening to share his or her baby book or other photos and reminisce about his or her story from arrival to now.

The Conversation: Discuss best memories, worst memories, old friends, teachers. Use the questions as prompters to get to know each other before you met.

Tips: Some of us have had less than happy childhoods. Don't pressure for more or deeper information than the other wants to share. This should be a fun time, so far as possible. Emphasize the positive, and celebrate God's hand at work in and through your pasts.

A. Welcome to the world

- Where were you born, and what were the circumstances?
- How did you get your name and why?
- How did the rest of the family receive you?
- Were you cute, funny-looking, sweet or cranky, active or given to pondering great mysteries?

B. Off to school (and other adventures)

- What are your earliest memories?
- How did you handle the first day of school?

- Who were your favorite teachers and subjects?
- Who were your best friends?
- How were you disciplined?
- How did you get along with parents?
- What did you dream of becoming when you were little?

C. Deeper questions for you and me...

- When did you first put your faith in Jesus?
- What were the saddest and happiest points in your childhood?
- How did you change during adolescence and high school?
- Looking back now, how do you see God at work in your life to now?

Courtship Conversation

#2

WHO'S COOKING TONIGHT?

The Date: Trade evenings, probably at least a week apart. Your assignment includes planning the menu, shopping, table-setting, cooking, and cleanup. The meal can be as simple or as splendid as you wish. The purpose is to have fun and stimulate a good conversation, not to compete for top chef honors.

The Conversation: Use this date to talk about your past experiences and current expectations when it comes to gender roles as they relate to household duties.

Tips: You might want to save the discussion for after dinner (don't distract the cook). Refer to chapter 7 of this book, "If Boys Would Be Men, Would Girls Be Ladies?" for insights about this topic.

A. In the kitchen when you were growing up:

- Who did the cooking?
- Did he or she get creative or festive—or just get food on the table?
- What meal or meals did your family sit down together at on a regular basis?
- What was mealtime like as a family experience?
- Who cleaned up and why?

B. What about other chores?

- Who did the most housecleaning?
- Who did the grocery shopping?
- Who took care of the yard?
- Who took care of the car(s)?
- How well did the parent accomplish these tasks?
- What were family attitudes about these tasks?

C. Now that we have some food for thought...

- What around the house would you want to do differently from your family?
- Do you believe God has given unique roles to husband and wife in marriage? How would you sum up the Bible's teaching?
- When you read chapter 7, were there any parts you reacted to or disagreed with?
- What are some advantages to God's plan for clear roles for husband and wife?

Courtship Conversation

#3

DO YOU BOGGLE?

The Date: Play a competitive game with some high stakes attached (a fun prize). If you can't agree on the game, play his and then hers.

The Conversation: Discuss competitiveness and attitudes toward winning. Also, what is the history of family fun and games for each person?

Tips: Games that reveal the most about how we play or compete are those that leave a lot open to interpretation: "Is that *really* a word?" or "Hey! You're not allowed to point!" If you'd rather include other people, that works too. Tackle these questions in a relaxed setting (a walk, sitting by a fire) after the fun is over.

A. Your history with games:

- What sports or games did you most enjoy growing up?
- How much did winning matter? (Be honest!)
- What were you taught about winning and losing by coaches, teachers, and your parents?
- What kind of sportsmanship was modeled for you?

B. How do you feel?

- Would you describe yourself as competitive? Why or why not?
- Have you ever become angry while playing a game with a friend or relative? If so, what happened, how was the relationship affected, and how were things resolved?
- Do you prefer games of chance or games of skill?
- How important do you think it is for families to play games or to recreate together?
- Are you happy to play games you tend to lose at?
- Have you ever cheated at a game? What happened?
- How important is it for others to be enjoying themselves for you to have fun playing?
- Do you prefer to play with a team or on your own?

C. Now that we've played together...

Take some time to think through together what you think you learned, or can learn, from playing games and other kinds of competitive recreation. For example, about:

- A sense of humor
- Graciousness—or lack of it
- A capacity for compromise and cooperation
- Attitudes about conflict
- Feelings about fairness and tolerance for perceived injustice

Courtship Conversation

#4

SUNDAY MORNING SURPRISE

The Date: Visit a Christian church that takes a significantly different approach from the one you're both used to. Then go for lunch or coffee to talk. (If possible, try to make this happen wtihout missing worship at your home church.)

The Conversation: Ask the question, What do we really believe—and why? Discuss worship styles, core beliefs, and God's purpose for the church. What your family of origin believed. What your expectations for your future family will be in terms of participation, attendance, and commitment.

Tips: Reading *Stop Dating the Church* might help to spark ideas and give you an additional context for the discussion.

A. Your history with church:

- How did your family approach church while you were growing up?
- How did your feelings about or enthusiasm for church change over the years?
- How much did church shape your ideas about God? What else shaped them?
- What kinds of experiences have you had with different forms of worship or styles of churches? What did you learn?

- What was your worst experience with a church, if you had one, and why?

B. What matters most:

- What do you think are the most important qualities in a church?
- Was there anything about the church you just attended that you liked a lot? Didn't like?
- Do you expect to be highly involved in church all your life?
- What will your expectations or requirements be for your children's attendance?

C. Soul and spirit for you and me...

- How important is worship to you, personally and corporately?
- How important is a regular personal devotional time (prayer and Bible reading, study)?
- How closely do you think a couple's beliefs should match?
- What are your biggest seemingly unanswerable questions about God or Christianity?
- In which area of your Christian life do you feel that you want or need to grow the most?
- What aspects of your Christian life and relationship to God would you say have changed the most in the past year?

Courtship Conversation

#5

IT TAKES TWO

The Date: Come up with a craft or building project that requires the two of you to work closely together within a limited time frame.

The Conversation: Discuss how you each like to approach a complex task or creative challenge. How well you work together on a task under stress—one definition of marriage—might be enlightening!

Tips: Approach the project with no predetermined leader or decision maker. See what roles you naturally fall into, and notice how the process unfolds. That's part of the fun. Wait until the job is done to get together and discuss these questions.

A. What's your work history?

- In the past, what was the greatest creative or academic task you faced? How did you approach it? What was the outcome?
- What was the most demanding physical work you ever participated in? Was it a positive experience or not? Why?
- What kind of work attitudes were modeled in your home?

B. What's your work style?

- Do you get easily frustrated when things go wrong, or are you usually patient?
- Do you tend to procrastinate, or do you like to work ahead?
- Do you prefer to read directions beforehand or wait until you're stuck?
- Do you prefer to work alone or with others?
- Do you care more about getting it right or getting it done?

C. When we worked on this project together...

- Who was the decision maker? How was that decided?
- Were there moments of stress? If so, when and why?
- Would you say we complemented one another or not? Did it slow us down or speed us up to share the task?
- Was there any joking or poking fun at one another? Okay or not?
- What did we learn about each other's approach to a project?
- Did you enjoy the opportunity to work together?

Courtship Conversation

#6

KIDS ON THE LOOSE

The Date: Babysit for a family with plenty of children. Make sure it includes preparing their dinner and getting them all to bed.

The Conversation: Soon after this date, get together to discuss the experience, share your history regarding parenting styles and your views about raising kids.

Tips: Follow up on answers until you've covered all the key implications. But be comfortable with some vagueness or "I don't know's," too—this is not a test!

A. About my mom and dad...

- How did your parents approach discipline—and who was the primary disciplinarian?
- What was most often used to motivate—reward or threat of punishment?
- Were the boundaries and rules clear?
- How often did your parents yell or raise their voices at the kids?
- How consistent were your parents' dealings with you and your siblings?
- Did your parents present a united front?
- Was your dad the clear spiritual leader of the home?

B. What I believe:

- What does the Bible say about the different roles of a mom and dad?
- How important is it to you that the person you marry shares the same parenting values and views?
- How do you feel about discipline and who should administer it?
- What mistake do you *most* fear making as a parent?
- How would you describe a parent's most important role? His or her most important goal?

C. About the other night (when we babysat)...

- What was the most challenging part of the evening?
- Did anything surprise you?
- Which of us felt the most comfortable, and why?
- How did the kids respond to each of us? Were there any "tests"?
- Did we operate as a unit or divide up roles and duties?
- Did you think we agreed about how to handle stressful situations?
- Do you think we would enjoy raising children together?

Courtship Conversation

#7

SHOW ME THE MONEY

The Date: Decide together where you can get the best dinner for two for under ten dollars.

The Conversation: Discuss your parents' financial priorities, how you approach budgeting and money, and what you hope for down the road.

Tips: Try to be as honest as possible about this difficult issue.

A. The way it was:

- How did your parents seem to approach budgeting?
  - carefully and with a plan
  - on a wing and a prayer
  - I have no idea

- Which would you say each of your parents valued more:
  - security (saving)?
  - gratification (spending)?

- What lessons did they teach you about money? Were these by example or by word? Intentional or unintentional?

- Did your parents connect their finances with their spiritual life by tithing or giving? If so, how, and what were some results?

- Was financial hardship endured or celebrated creatively?
- Did your parents argue about finances?
- How aware were you of your family's financial state?

B. The way it is:

- How do you feel about money in general? Is it a gift or a burden?
- Do you keep a careful record of finances or hope there's money in the account?
- Name three important biblical truths about money.
- How do you feel about credit cards and debt?
- Do you believe that you get what you pay for or that being thrifty pays off? (Do you dart for the designer labels or the sale rack?)

C. Down the road for us...

- What standard of living would you hope to enjoy in the long-term?
- Do you think a husband should have the final say in major financial decisions, or should all decisions be mutual?
- Do you see the wife working and bringing in an income even after she has kids? Part-time or full-time?
- Describe the approach to money and budgeting that you ideally hope to share with a mate someday.

Courtship Conversation

#8

STILL GOING STRONG

The Date: Go to lunch or dinner with a longtime married couple.

The Conversation: What are their secrets to success? What do they regret? Later, discuss what you learned from this couple as well as from the marriages you know best. Also, this is a good time to talk about biblical roles and priorities as described in, for example, Ephesians 5:21–33.

Tips: Talk together before the dinner about the kinds of questions you'd like to ask and feel comfortable broaching. Have some fun predicting answers. Does he snore? Does she ever get shrill? Have they ever argued for hours?

A. What makes a marriage last?

- Why do you think over half of marriages (including among Christians) end in divorce?
- What seems to be the most important ingredient to a long marriage (apart from issues of Christian belief and experience)?
- What is more important—romance or respect? (This is a trick question!)

B. What do you believe?

- How do you define a wife's "submission" or "reverence" as it's discussed in Ephesians?
- What is your definition of a husband's leadership or being the "spiritual head"?
- How important do you believe these roles are to the success of a marriage? Why?
- How important is romance, or "being in love"?
- Under what circumstances is divorce a biblical option?
- What would you say to a couple who is on the brink of divorce?

C. About the couple we had dinner with...

- What, if anything, surprised us?
- Has the marriage endured hardships that might have broken some couples? What were they?
- How did they interact with one another at the meal?
- What part did their spiritual life seem to play in their staying together?
- Does the couple subscribe to traditional biblical roles or something else?
- Do we think they are still "in love"?
- What was the best piece of advice or most insightful comment they made?
- What would you most want a courting couple to say about your marriage when *you* are the "old married couple" who gets invited to dinner?

NOTES

Chapter 3

Eugene Peterson, "Introduction to Proverbs," in *The Message* (Colorado Springs, Colo.: Navpress, 1993), 862.

Chapter 4

John Calvin, *Calvin Institutes of the Christian Religion I*, ed. John T. McNeill (Philadelphia, Penn.: Westminster Press, 1960).

C. S. Lewis in Dr. Bruce Waltke, *Finding the Will of God* (Gresham, Ore.: Vision House Publishing, 1995), 31.

Kin Hubbard, "Lack o' Pep," in Abe Martin, *Hoss Sense and Nonsense* (1926), 19.

L. M. Montgomery, *Anne of Avonlea* (New York: Harper and Row, 1985), 277.

Chapter 6

Matthew Henry, *Commentary on Genesis,* quoted in the Spring 1999 issue of the *Council on Biblical Manhood and Womanhood Newsletter,* P.O. Box 7337, Libertyville, IL 60048.

Elisabeth Elliot, *The Mark of a Man* (Grand Rapids, Mich.: Fleming H. Revell, 1981), 13.

John Stott, in Alexander Strauch, *Men and Women, Equal Yet Different* (Littleton, Colo.: Lewis and Roth Publishers, 1999), 76.

Elliot, *The Mark of a Man,* 158.

Chapter 7

Gary and Betsy Ricucci, *Love That Lasts* (Gaithersburg, Md.: PDI Communications, 1992), 28. Used with permission.

Chapter 8

"All in a Day's Work," *Reader's Digest,* October 1999.

Chapter 9

Douglas Jones, "Worshiping with Body," *Credenda Agenda,* vol. 10, no. 2.

John MacArthur, *Commentary on Hebrews,* quoted in Deborah Belonick, "Safe Sex Isn't Always Safe for the Soul," www.beliefnet.com.

John White, *Eros Defiled* (Downers Grove, Ill.: InterVarsity Press, 1977), 53.

Bethany Torode, "(Don't) Kiss Me," originally published by *Boundless Webzine,* www.boundless.org. Used by permission.

Chapter 10

Joni Eareckson Tada and Steven Estes, *When God Weeps* (Grand Rapids, Mich.: Zondervan Publishing House, 1997), 52–54. Used by permission.

Rebecca Pippert, *Hope Has Its Reasons* (New York: Guideposts, 1989), 102–4. Used by permission.

John Stott, *The Cross* (Downers Grove, Ill.: Intervarsity Press, 1986), 60–61.

Ibid., 12.

Jay Adams, *From Forgiven to Forgiving* (Amityville, N.Y.: Calvary Press, 1994), 12.

David Boehi, Brent Nelson, Jeff Schulte, and Lloyd Shadrach, *Preparing for Marriage,* ed. Dennis Rainey (Ventura, Calif.: Gospel Light, 1997), 226–29.

Chapter 11

David Powlison and John Yenchko, "Should We Get Married?" *Journal of Biblical Counseling* 14 (Spring 1996): 42. For sub-

scription information, call (215) 884-7676 or visit
www.ccef.org. David Powlison and John Yenchko's article is
available as a booklet and is entitled *Pre-Engagement: 5
Questions to Ask Yourselves.* To order, contact Resources for
Changing Lives, 1803 E. Willow Grove Ave., Glenside, PA
19038 or call (800) 318-2186.

Eva McAllaster in *Recovering Biblical Manhood and Womanhood,*
ed. John Piper and Wayne Grudem (Wheaton, Ill: Crossway
Books, 1991), xxii.

Chapter 12

Mike Mason, *The Mystery of Marriage: As Iron Sharpens Iron*
(Sisters, Ore.: Multnomah Books, 1985), 74.

ACKNOWLEDGMENTS

I am very grateful to the many people who helped make this book possible—both in its original form and for this updated edition. Thanks to David Sacks, Carolyn McCulley, Jon Ward, Cara Wilcox, Eric Hughes, Jeff Purswell, John Loftness, Marie Silard, Janelle Bradshaw, Rich and Christy Shipe, Travis and Jonalee Earles, David Powlison, John Yenchko, Bob and Julie Kauflin, Kerrin and Megan Russell, Debbie Partlow, Don Jacobson, Kevin Marks, and Doug Gabbert.

Nicole Whitacre worked diligently as my research assistant.

C. J. Mahaney's friendship and care touched every part of this book. His helpful critique and encouragement were essential throughout.

David and Heather Kopp were patient and faithful friends in the labor of writing. And I am very grateful for their work in creating the "Courtship Conversations."

My parents, Gregg and Sono, read the first draft and were willing to tell me that it stank. It really did. My mother's prayers and thoughtful calls encouraged me so much. My father's willingness to drop everything to read chapters demonstrated his love for me.

My deepest appreciation is reserved for Shannon, my lover and my best friend. She is the one person who truly sacrificed of herself while I wrote. And her humility and willingness to share her story so that others could be encouraged is the most powerful part of this book. After this book was first released, letters poured in from men and women who dared to hope again in the transforming power of God's grace because of Shannon's story. I pray that many more will look to the Cross and find forgiveness through the example of my precious wife. I am more amazed today than ever that God gave her to me.

ABOUT THE AUTHOR

Joshua Harris got his start in writing as the editor of *New Attitude*, a Christian magazine for home-school teens. He wrote his first book *I Kissed Dating Goodbye* at age 21. In 1997 Joshua moved from Oregon to Gaithersburg, Maryland, to be trained for pastoral ministry at Covenant Life Church. It was there—five years after giving up the dating game himself—that Joshua met, courted, and married his bride, Shannon. In the fall of 2004 Joshua assumed the role of senior pastor at Covenant Life Church. He also leads a national conference called NEXT, whose goal is to see the gospel transferred to the next generation.

Joshua is also the author of *Boy Meets Girl: Say Hello to Courtship,* *Sex is Not the Problem (Lust Is),* and *Stop Dating the Church!* Joshua and his wife Shannon just celebrated their ten-year anniversary. They have three children, Emma, Joshua Quinn and Mary Kate.

For information about Joshua's work, his speaking schedule and free online sermons visit his Web site at: www.joshharris.com.

Connect with Joshua Harris
joshharris.com
Facebook • Twitter

REDISCOVER
the relevance and power
of Christian truth in your life

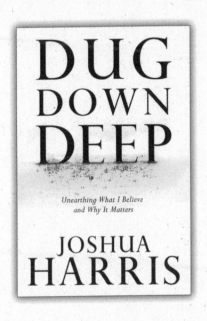

With humor and engaging reflections on Christian beliefs, Harris shows that orthodoxy isn't just for scholars—it is for anyone who longs to know the living Jesus Christ. Whether you are just exploring Christianity or you are a veteran believer finding yourself overly familiar and cold-hearted, *Dug Down Deep* will help you rediscover the timeless truths of Scripture.

"Theology matters because if we get it wrong then our whole life will be wrong."
— Joshua Harris

The long-awaited release.
Available January 2010.

Ready to Rethink Dating?

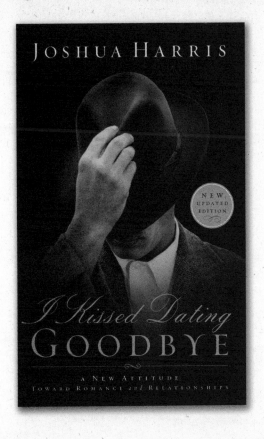

Going out? Been dumped? Waiting for a call that doesn't come? Have you tasted pain in dating, drifted through one romance or, possibly, several of them? Ever wondered, *Isn't there a better way*?

I Kissed Dating Goodbye shows what it means to entrust your love life to God. Joshua Harris shares his story of giving up dating and discovering that God has something even better—a life of sincere love, true purity, and purposeful singleness.

Are You Dating the Church?

We are a generation of consumers, independent and critical. We attend church, but we don't want to settle down and truly invest ourselves. We're not into commitment—we only want to date the church. Is this what God wants for us?

Stop Dating the Church reminds us that faith was never meant to be a solo pursuit. The church is the place where God grows us, encourages us, and uses us best. Loving Jesus Christ involves a passionate commitment to His church—around the world and down the street. We can't be apathetic. It's time to fall in love with the family of God.

Purity in the Real World

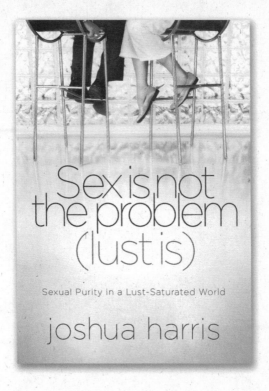

Lust wants to twist your natural sexual desires into something destructive. God can free you to live in purity and true joy. This refreshingly honest book helps men and women face the daily reality of sexual temptation. Forthright without being graphic, it covers topics like entertainment and media, how to use Scripture to fight the lies of lust, and how Christians should deal with masturbation.

"For your joy and Christ's honor, I commend this book to you. It is realistic, practical, and hope-giving."

—John Piper